Savings Bond Advisor
Fifth Edition

Tom Adams

Alert Media
New York

Savings Bond Advisor
Fifth Edition

Alert Media – New York

email: savings-bond-advisor@alert-media.com

web: http://www.alert-media.com/

Information in this book is subject to change without notice. Updated information and links mentioned in the text are available on our web site at:

http://www.Savings-Bond-Advisor.com/

ISBN-13: 978-0-9760645-3-4
ISBN-10: 0-9760645-3-7

ISSN: 1552-1249 (#5.0)

The Vanguard Group, Inc. offers the Vanguard 500 Index fund. Standard & Poor's®, S&P®, S&P 500®, Standard & Poor's 500® and 500® are trademarks of The McGraw-Hill Companies, Inc.

Dedicated to
Joseph C. Weishaar

Acknowledgements: We are indebted to the Treasury's Bureau of Public Debt – particularly its Public Affairs and Customer Service personnel, who have patiently answered our many questions. There are many others we have learned from and been encouraged by through the years. Heartfelt thanks to all.

Table of Contents

Part I – Creating Your Investment

Part II – Managing Your Investment

Part III – Redeeming Your Investment

Introduction

Is this book for you?

Part 1 – Creating Your Investment

1 – An introduction to Savings Bonds

2 – Why Savings Bonds?

3 – Today's choices – Series I and Series EE

4 – How to invest in Savings Bonds

5 – Whose name goes on the bond?

6 – All about TreasuryDirect

Part II – Managing your investment

Part III – Redeeming your investment

Is this book for you?

What savvy investors are up to now

Lose the commissions and fees

Do you want to know a secret?

Getting the most from this book

Getting the most from our web site

What savvy investors are up to now

Investors like you read books. In addition to this one, two other important investment books are **Fooled by Randomness**, by Nassim Taleb, and **Unexpected Returns**, by Ed Easterling.

The essence of **Fooled by Randomness** is that most of what passes for investment expertise is just good luck – and good luck eventually changes to bad luck.

If you want to get out of the luck business, your investment strategy has to put more importance on protecting yourself from losses than on obtaining the highest returns.

The essence of **Unexpected Returns** is that markets run in long-term boom and bust cycles. The 20 years from 1980 to 2000 saw falling inflation, falling interest rates, and booming stock and bond prices.

But the long-term trend will run the other way for the next 5 to 20 years. If inflation and interest rates are headed up and stocks and bonds are headed down, where should you invest the money you're saving?

A hedge fund is a possibility. Hedge funds are all about managing risk. But the hedge fund industry is unregulated, the managers take 20% off the top of earnings each year, returns are shrinking as more hedge funds enter the market, and the minimum investment is $1 million.

If you can't afford or don't like hedge funds, but you like the idea of hedging – of giving up the highest possible return in exchange for almost complete certainty that you can't lose your money – then this book, **Savings Bond Advisor**, is for you.

It explains how small investors can use one of the safest of all securities, Series I Savings Bonds issued by the U.S. Treasury, to create an investment portfolio that is always growing, never shrinking.

Figure P-1 demonstrates exactly how this works. It assumes you've invested an equal amount of money every month – this is the best way to invest – in both Series I Savings Bonds and the Vanguard 500 index fund.

As stock funds go, the Vanguard 500 fund is one of the largest and most respected. As an index fund, it tries to match the performance of the Standard and Poor's 500 stock index. This index is made up of the stocks of the largest companies in the U.S. and they are weighted in the index by their size.

The thin, straight line shows how much money has been invested. It goes up very steadily because an equal amount of money is added each month.

The upper line is the total value of the Series I Savings Bond investment. Note that this line always goes up. As time goes on, the spread between it and the amount invested widens. This is compound, inflation-adjusted interest talking.

The line that goes both up and down is the total value of the stock market investment, including reinvested dividends. Note that if you were forced to cash in this investment between 2001 and 2003, you wouldn't even have gotten back what you put in.

I update Figure I-1 monthly. To see the latest version, go to our web site, click on Book Notes, and pick Note I-1.

Savings Bonds take away that risk. You trade the *chance* of higher stock market returns for the *certainty* of getting back your entire investment, plus interest.

As you're about to learn, Savings Bonds can protect you from the risk of default, the risk of inflation, the risk of capital loss, and they have tax advantages. In today's environment, this is the best place for money you can't afford to lose.

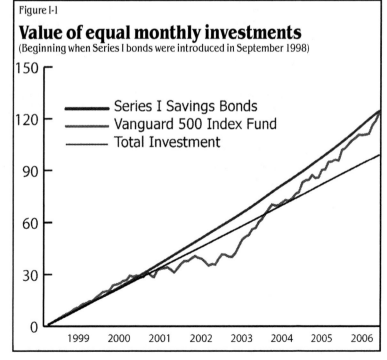

Figure I-1

Value of equal monthly investments
(Beginning when Series I bonds were introduced in September 1998)

— Series I Savings Bonds
— Vanguard 500 Index Fund
— Total Investment

Lose the commissions and fees

Nonetheless, most financial professionals don't recommend Savings Bonds. If you find one who does, listen carefully, because you're finally hearing more than just a commission talking.

Compared to the smart and sophisticated investments that financial professionals earn commissions on, Savings Bonds are a do-it-yourself, low-cost investment.

But seven out of ten Savings Bond investors earn less than they could have – either because they're not paying attention or because their investment doesn't work the way they think it does.

Here are the four major money-losing mistakes that Savings Bond investors make:

★ losing earnings by holding stinkers (bonds that have stopped earning interest), either in a futile attempt to avoid income tax or out of sheer ignorance that some of their holdings have a distinct aroma

★ missing maximum returns by buying the wrong bonds, by redeeming the wrong bonds, or by redeeming the right bonds at the wrong time

★ paying too much income tax by not having a plan to minimize taxes and by filling out tax forms incorrectly

★ wasting your family's money on legal fees and taxes by ignoring the estate planning benefits of Savings Bonds

The more Savings Bonds you have, the larger and more costly these mistakes become. But it's not hard to avoid them. This book tells you how.

A do-it-yourself Savings Bond investment has a lot less risk and a return that compares favorably with the average investment that you can get from a commissioned professional.

Do you want to know a secret?

About 55 million individuals own Savings Bonds. Since the U.S. population is now approaching 300 million, only about one in six Americans own Savings Bonds.

If they've heard of them at all, the five-out-of-six believe that Savings Bonds are a frumpy, old-fashioned investment. We aren't bombarded with Savings Bond advertising as we are for investments that pay sales fees and commissions.

Moreover, many of the people who don't own Savings Bonds and who know little about them are the financial professionals who write books and offer personal advice.

If you're reading this page in a bookstore, look in the index of any of the books on the shelf in front of you. You'll discover that most financial advice books don't even have an index entry for Savings Bonds.

What's worse, many of these same advisors are certain they know how Savings Bonds work, but what they know hasn't been true for years (if was ever true at all).

Moreover, of the Americans who do own Savings Bonds, most have just one or two that they received as gifts or prizes. Often these bonds have more emotional than financial value. And these folks figure all other Savings Bond owners are just like them.

However, the total amount invested in Savings Bonds is over $200,000 million. Given the 80-20 rule, the 11 million Americans with the largest Savings Bond holdings are systematic savers who have, on average, an investment of over $14,500 each.

Although you hardly ever hear investment professionals talk about Savings Bonds – and when they do they're often spouting misinformation – Savings Bonds are the secret of millions and millions of American investors. You're in good company.

Getting the most from this book

You can use this book to learn about Savings Bonds by reading it straight through or you can use it as a reference tool.

Begin at the table of contents – the book has four parts:
★ Part I – Creating Your Investment
★ Part II – Managing Your Investment
★ Part III – Redeeming Your Investment

This structure follows the phases of the investment cycle.

Information that's critical to those putting money into Savings Bonds is pretty different from the information that's critical to those who are managing a large Savings Bond investment, which is different from the information you'll need when you're ready to take money out.

This allows you to concentrate on the part of the book that concerns the phase of the investment cycle you're in.

Watch for notes in this part of the page. They will highlight or expand on the page's main idea and will often point you toward additional or more current information on our web site.

Getting the most from our web site

Centered at the bottom of every page of this book is the URL of our web site, ***www.Savings-Bond-Advisor.com***.

The book and the web site work together to give you a better experience than either can alone.

For example, the Treasury changes Savings Bonds interest rates twice a year; rates of competing investments change daily. We always have current rates available on the web site.

Go to the web site now, add it to your Favorites or Bookmarks, and take a look around.

The link at the upper-right labelled *Book Notes* takes you to a page of web links. First click on *Book Notes*, then click on *Fifth Edition*, which leads to the notes for this edition of the book.

To see how this works, flip back and look at the text in the right hand margin on page 7. The text refers to *Book Note 1-1*. On the page that comes up after you click on *Fifth Edition*, find Note 1-1 and click on it. There's an updated, color version of that graph!

This system means you don't have to type in URLs from the book. Instead, just click on the links on the Fifth Edition's Book Notes page. If a URL changes or I make a mistake, I can fix it.

While you're visiting the web site, subscribe to my free Savings Bond email alerts. This allows you to be among the first to know when interest rates change or other significant Savings Bond news happens.

The web site includes a link you can use to send me questions, comments, or feedback. If you've purchased this book, I'll respond to any additional questions you have by email.

After removing all information that would identify you, I post some of the questions I receive with my answers on the site. You can subscribe to the web site's RSS feed to keep up to date with Savings Bond news and new questions and answers.

Don't miss our free email alert service. I don't bombard you with emails – I only send you something where there's news to report. Typically I send about 12 issues a year. It's an easy way for you to get important updates on changes to the Savings Bond program.

Part 1 –
Creating Your Investment

An introduction to Savings Bonds

Why Savings Bonds?

Today's choices – Series I and Series EE

How to invest in Savings Bonds

Whose name goes on the bond?

All about TreasuryDirect

Chapter 1

An introduction to Savings Bonds

The top five misconceptions about Savings Bonds

Basic features of today's Savings Bonds

The top five misconceptions about Savings Bonds

Misconceptions and misinformation are the hallmark of discussions about Savings Bonds. Although they are an excellent choice for the low-risk portion of your investment portfolio, Savings Bonds aren't quite like any other investment.

As the word *savings* indicates, they have some features of bank savings accounts, such as they way they earn compound interest.

As the word *bonds* indicates, they have some features of corporate and government bonds, such as they way they are registered to specific owners.

They are also similar to bank certificates of deposit, in that they have early withdrawal penalties and that you can purchase and redeem them either at a brick and mortar bank or using an online account.

And like retirement savings plans such as 401Ks and IRAs, they allow you to defer income taxes on your earnings.

But while Savings Bonds share some features with other investment choices, in the end there's nothing else that works like a Savings Bond. This causes lots of misconceptions.

Let's begin by looking at the major misconceptions one by one, in Dave Letterman order:

Misconception #5 – You can't redeem a Savings Bond until it matures

While it's true that some competing investments can't be cashed until they mature, Savings Bonds can be cashed after one year.

There is a penalty of the most recent three months of interest if cashed before five years. All of the new bonds being issued today pay interest for 30 years. Depending on the Series, older Savings Bonds pay interest for 20 or 30 years.

Misconception #4 – You earn interest on the face value of a Savings Bond, not on what it's worth

The paper Series EE Savings Bonds you buy at a bank are issued at half of their face value. This means you pay, for example, $50 for a bond that says $100 on it.

Most people think this means something, but in fact it means nothing at all. Even a broken clock is right twice a day, but it's extremely rare for a Series EE bond to be worth exactly its face value.

These bonds, like all other Savings Bonds (none of which have this feature), are always worth:
★ what you invested, plus
★ what your investment has earned in interest, plus
★ what your accumulated interest has earned in interest

Series EE bonds are guaranteed to double in value in a certain number of years. The number of years changes as interest rates rise and fall. That's the source of the marketing gimmick of putting a value that's double your investment on the bonds.

But it's just a marketing gimmick. It has caused so much confusion the Treasury has stopped using it except on paper EE bonds.

You earn interest on the amount you invested and your accumulated interest – no matter what series your bonds are; no matter if they are paper or electronic.

Misconception #3 – You're better off holding Savings Bonds that have stopped earning interest than redeeming them and being forced to pay the income tax you owe

Savings Bonds come with a retirement-account-like tax-deferral feature – the IRS allows you to defer the interest you earn for tax purposes until you receive it in cash or your bond stops earning interest.

There are ways to minimize the income tax you pay. But these methods require attention to your investment and advance planning. In Chapter 17 I'll lead you through the tax issues and strategies of Savings Bonds.

But, as we'll see in Chapter 17, unless your income is low enough to take advantage of the Savings Bond education deduction, or unless your income is high enough that your are willing to give all your Savings Bond interest to a recognized charity, federal income tax on the interest you've earned will eventually be paid by either you or your heirs.

But some investors are so tax-averse that rather than paying the tax they owe, they hold on to Savings Bonds that have stopped earning interest. This is such a bad idea I've started calling these earnings-free bonds *stinker bonds*.

The Treasury actually has a small team of people that tries to contact owners of these bonds to let them know their money hasn't been claimed.

- Yet seven out of ten investors the team reaches say they don't want to cash the bonds because they'll have to pay income tax on the interest they've earned.

The Treasury's unclaimed-bond team is so small and the amount of unclaimed bonds is so large they don't even try to contact people who have a common name or a small amount of unclaimed bonds.

From a financial perspective, holding on to stinkers is an appallingly bad decision. Most people quickly lose more by giving the government an interest-free loan than they'll ever gain by delaying their tax due date.

Please recognise that either you or your heirs *are going to pay the tax someday.* The only alternative is to just let the Treasury have your investment in perpetuity, which means the government gets 100% of your money instead of 10% to 35%.

When you factor in inflation, stinker bonds are losing money every month.

If your plan is to leave the taxes to your heirs, not only will you lose the interest you could have earned, their tax rate will probably be higher than yours, costing your family even more money.

And don't be fooled into thinking your heirs can avoid taxes by taking advantage of the *stepped-up-basis* rule (see Chapter 10). That rule applies only to capital gains; Savings Bonds earn interest and don't have capital gains.

But wait – there's more. The IRS says you actually owe the income tax in the year Savings Bonds stop earning interest – whether you cash them or not. By holding stinkers you're setting yourself up for an amended return for a previous year along with back taxes and penalties.

If you have Saving Bonds that have stopped earning interest, redeem them, pay your tax with some of the money, and use the rest to buy new bonds. Your family will end up with far more money than you'll ever get by holding on to dead and rotting stinkers.

And if you have Savings Bonds that aren't stinkers yet, let me give you an advance hint about what you'll learn in Chapter 17 – the best tax savings go to those who make a plan years in advance and redeem and reinvest their bonds over a multi-year period.

Misconception #2 – Savings Bonds earn lousy rates

There is no safer investment than Savings Bonds. Since the rate you earn is related to the amount of risk you're willing take, the interest rates that Savings Bonds pay are indeed lousy compared to what you get if you're lucky enough to actually get the top return of a riskier investment.

On the other hand, Savings Bond rates aren't lousy at all compared to what you get if you risk and lose, or even if you risk and come out even.

Compared to other low-risk investments, the Savings Bond rate is usually very competitive. However, since the Treasury puts a rate on Savings Bonds that's good for six months, while interest rates change every day, there are times when competitive investments have much better rates and times when they have much worse rates.

Overall, Savings Bonds earn solid, low-risk rates.

Misconception #1 – Good advice about Savings Bonds is easy to get

Traditionally, if you wanted to initiate a Savings Bond transaction, such as buying a bond or redeeming one, you went to a financial institution – a bank, savings and loan, or credit union.

Although there's now also an online alternative, which we'll discuss in Chapter 6, financial institutions are still the main place people initiate Savings Bond transactions today.

Consequently, people assume that bank tellers can advise them about Savings Bonds. And, in fact, a few bank tellers know Savings Bonds inside and out.

But because banks receive only a small handling fee from the Treasury for each Savings Bond transaction, they have no incentive to train their employees about Savings Bonds.

Banks can handle simple Savings Bond transactions, but they aren't trained to provide advice. Savings Bonds aren't a bank product. Your banker would rather see you invest in the bank's own certificates of deposit.

Savings Bonds are issued by the Savings Bond Division of the Bureau of Public Debt, which is a part of the U.S. Treasury. In this book I'll shorten all that to *the Treasury*.

It's also not unusual to find erroneous articles about Savings Bonds in newspapers, magazines, or on web sites. This is because reporters write articles by consulting experts.

But sometimes the expert sources for financial stories:

★ don't own Savings Bonds

★ don't have any incentive to learn about Savings Bonds, because they can't make a commission selling them

The Savings Bond Informer asked 400 banks five common questions about Savings Bonds. Only four banks (1%) answered all five questions correctly, although about half answered "boldly and inaccurately," as if they knew the correct answer.

★ think Savings Bonds are a simple, easily-understood investment, when in fact they have a wide variety of somewhat
confusing characteristics, which depend on an individual
bond's series and issue date.

Good advice about Savings Bonds is hard to get.

The Treasury has a Savings Bonds web site at *http://www.
treasurydirect.gov/* that is the ultimate source for Savings Bond
information. However, while the Treasury provides all the facts, it
doesn't provide much in the way of advice.

Basic features of today's Savings Bonds

The Savings Bonds you can buy today have the following features. We'll spend as much as entire chapters discussing some of these features later, but for now you'll benefit from a high fly-over:

Guaranteed by the U.S. Treasury

All Savings Bonds are issued by the U.S. Treasury and backed by the full faith and credit of the U.S. government, making them among the safest of all investments.

No risk of capital loss

Unlike traditional corporate and government bonds, you can't get back less than you paid for Savings Bonds. The value of traditional bonds and bond mutual funds goes down when interest rates go up. While you can get all of your money back by holding a traditional bond until it stops paying interest, you can lose money if you need to redeem it before it matures. This won't happen with Savings Bonds.

Likewise, unfortunately, there is no possibility of capital gains when interest rates go down, as there is with traditional bonds and bond mutual funds.

Two series – Series I and Series EE

The Treasury's Savings Bond product line currently has two options, Series I and Series EE. We'll discuss the differences in the next chapter. Everything in this section applies to both series.

Two types – paper and electronic

In most states, most banks, credit unions, and similar financial institutions will process purchase and redemption transactions for the traditional paper (or *definitive*) Savings Bonds. Paper bonds are available in $50, $75, $100, $200, $500, $1,000, $5,000, and $10,000 denominations.

Electronic (or *book*) Savings Bonds can be purchased and redeemed online by opening an account with TreasuryDirect. You can invest any amount, to the penny, from $25 up to your annual investment limit.

Tax advantages

Federal income tax can be *deferred* on Savings Bond interest until you redeem the bond. Savings Bond interest is exempt from state and local income taxes. If you have higher education expenses, you may qualify to exclude your Savings Bond interest from your Federal income tax.

Investment limits

Savings Bonds can be purchased for as little as $25. This compares to the minimum investment of $1,000 for most competing investments.

However, unlike other investments, there is a maximum limit on the amount you can invest in Savings Bonds in one calendar year.

The limit is $30,000 per Social Security Number, per series, per type, which creates an effective maximum investment of $120,000 per person per year ($30,000 each in Series I electronic, Series I paper, Series EE electronic, Series EE paper – with the Series EE paper having a face value of $60,000).

Redemption limits and penalties

With one exception for Treasury-recognized disasters, Savings Bonds can't be redeemed at all for one year. If redeemed before five years, you forfeit the last three months of interest earned, disaster or not.

Large denomination paper bonds can be partially redeemed – you'll receive cash and your choice of smaller denomination bonds with the same Series and issue date. Electronic bonds can be partially redeemed in any amount of $25 or more.

In case of a significant disaster, the Treasury will allow Savings Bonds to be redeemed during the first year. We announce these exceptions on our web site. See Book Note 1-1 for any currently open programs.

Final maturity after 30 years

Today's Savings Bonds stop earning interest after 30 years. All Series I and Series EE bonds that have ever been issued are currently earning interest.

Interest accrual and compounding

Interest on Savings Bonds is **compounded** twice a year and added to the value of the bond. This means interest earnings are calculated on both what you paid for the bond and the interest the bond has earned.

Interest on today's Savings Bonds **accrues** monthly. This means when you redeem a bond, you receive the interest earned through the first day of the month of redemption.

The month and year in which you buy a Savings Bond determines its issue date. All interest calculations assume you purchased the bond on the first day of that month – no matter which day the Treasury actually received your money.

Because Savings Bonds interest is always calculated as if you purchased the bond on the first day of the month, you can gain nearly an extra month's interest by timing your purchases to occur near the end of the month.

Likewise, when you redeem a bond, you should do it right after its value increases on the first day of the month. However, note that many older bonds accrue interest on a six-month schedule, rather than monthly. This creates a potential six-month redemption penalty. Find out how to avoid this penalty in Chapter 16.

The Treasury bases its interest calculations on a hypothetical $25 Savings Bond. Your investment is essentially divided into a set of imaginary small denomination bonds and you earn the rounded, calculated interest for the hypothetical bond times the number of hypothetical bonds your bond is equivalent to.

This calculation method magnifies the normal rounding errors and causes standard interest calculations to be too high or too low.

The Treasury does it this way so that someone who owns 200 $50 bonds earns exactly the same amount of interest as someone who owns one $10,000 bond. Since the rounding errors are random, there's nothing unfair or underhanded about the Treasury's calculation method.

Bonds in older Savings Bond series stop paying interest after 20 or 30 years, depending on the series.

The exact formula the Treasury uses to calculate interest is explained on our web site. See Book Note 1-2.

Zero-coupon

Coupon is a term that comes from the long-lost paper era, when corporate and government bonds were issued with tear-off coupons. Owners submitted the coupons to get their interest payments.

A zero-coupon bond is one in which interest payments are added to the value of the bond, rather than being paid in cash. This is how Savings Bonds and other investments that pay *compound interest* work.

Income securities

There are older types of Savings Bonds, called Series H and Series HH, that pay the interest you earn in cash rather than adding it to the value of the bond. I'll talk more about these in Chapter 7; they are no longer issued.

However, because TreasuryDirect has a partial withdrawal feature, you can effectively make Savings Bonds act like income securities by selling off a bit of your investment in your worst performing bonds each month.

This trick actually provides more flexibility than true income securities, since if you don't need the interest you can let it compound and if you need a bit more it's there for you.

If you have paper bonds, you can take advantage of this feature by converting them to TreasuryDirect's electronic bonds. I'll explain how in Chapter 6.

Ownership registration

All Savings Bonds Series are registered securities and registration is conclusive of ownership. This means that possession of a bond is meaningless – all that really counts is the name in the Treasury's records in West Virginia.

Because of these characteristics, Savings Bonds can't be used for collateral on a loan and they can't be given to charities without first cashing them in and paying taxes on the interest.

Non-marketable

Registration also means you can't buy or sell Savings Bonds from anyone but the U.S. Treasury or its agents. In most states, most banks and other financial institutions act as the Treasury's agents to help you buy and sell paper Savings Bonds, and the Treasury offers online Savings Bond accounts through TreasuryDirect.

Non-callable

The U.S. Treasury can't force you to redeem Savings Bonds before they stop paying interest at final maturity. Most interest-bearing investments work this way, but some fixed-rate bonds allow the issuer to call the bonds - which they typically do when interest rates fall.

No-load

Load refers to fees and commissions paid to those who sell you an investment. They are typically associated with mutual funds. There are never any fees for buying, selling, or holding Savings Bonds.

Serial Numbers and face values

The first letter in a paper Savings Bond's serial number will match its denomination:

- ★ L - $50
- ★ K - $75
- ★ C - $100
- ★ R - $200
- ★ D - $500
- ★ M - $1,000
- ★ V - $5,000
- ★ X - $10,000

Chapter 2

Why Savings Bonds?

Why save?

First stop paying interest, then start earning it

Anchor your portfolio with low-risk investments

Low-risk investment options

What's a marketable Treasury security?

Risks of Savings Bonds

Why save?

There are two primary reasons to save:

★ So that you can buy the things you want with money you already have rather than borrowing and paying interest.

★ So that you can even out your level of consumption over your lifetime.

Avoiding interest payments

Let me tell you about a very powerful financial technique – it's the foundation of the banking industry.

Borrow money at a low interest rate and lend it to people at a high interest rate.

The banking business doesn't amount to much more than borrow low, lend high, and it's huge.

Rather than supporting bankers, you can help yourself by avoiding interest payments. Unless you can get a very low interest, fixed-rate loan, such as a home mortgage, buy things with money you already have.

Sock away a significant portion of your income every month, buy things with your savings, and never pay interest.

You'll come out way ahead of your friends and relatives who borrow freely and end up spending a large part of their income on interest. How useless is that?

Leveling out your standard of living

The second reason to save is to avoid large dips in your standard of living over your lifetime. Most of us want to avoid having to make large reductions in our level of consumption. The only way to avoid this, particularly when your salary income drops after you retire, is through saving.

Calculating how much to save for retirement is a lot more complicated than the investment sales literature would have you believe.

Because Social Security will make up a larger proportion of their after-retirement income, those with relatively low incomes actually need to save a lower proportion of their income than those with higher incomes.

For a detailed analysis, I recommend **The Coming Generational Storm** by Lawrence J. Kotlikoff and Scott Burns. See Book Note 2-1 on our web site for an Amazon link to this book.

Kotlikoff and his colleagues have also written a software program that will help you answer the "how much to save for retirement" question. See our Book Note 2-2 for a link to his web site.

First stop paying interest, then start earning it

The way to get started is by saving back a significant part of your income each month.

If you aren't paying off your credit card bills in full, that is the best place to invest the money you're saving back. It doesn't make any sense to save money at an interest rate that's lower than what you're paying on your credit cards.

Once you've stopped contributing to the profits of the credit card companies, it's time to start putting the amount you're holding back into low-risk savings.

Don't be tempted at this point by investments that advertise high rates. The higher the rate, the higher the risk. As a beginning saver, you need to stick with low-risk investments.

The smaller your investment portfolio, the more of it you should keep in low-risk investments.

The low-risk portion should be able to replace your salary long enough to give you a satisfactory comfort level – financial counselors typically recommend a minimum of six months of your income.

So until you have half your annual salary safely saved, it doesn't make sense to even consider higher-risk investment options.

Anchor your portfolio with low-risk investments

No matter how large your investment portfolio and no matter how high your tolerance for risk, you should have a portion of your financial portfolio devoted to liquid, low-risk investments.

Liquidity means the *ability to quickly turn your investment into cash.* **Low-risk** means *no chance your investment will ever be worth less than what you've put into it.*

Sometimes you need access to your funds when the markets are down. In these situations you are forced to sell at a loss, which devastates your returns.

When you can't wait – when you need the money now for a down payment on a house, for a daughter's wedding, or to tide you through a layoff – you have to face the possibility of getting back less than you paid.

The best investment portfolios are diversified. Unless you have a working crystal ball and know how markets are going to perform in the future, your best bet is to split up your portfolio into investments with a variety of risk and reward levels.

Beginning investors should start with the low-risk anchor and move into building the higher-risk portions of their portfolios only after they have at least half a year of income covered.

Advanced investors should base their diversification strategy on their tolerance for risk, but should build the foundation of their portfolios on low-risk investments.

As we've seen since the stock market bubble burst, many investments can lose value drastically. But the value of Savings Bonds always goes up.

Low-risk investment options

Let's take a quick look at the world of low-risk investment options.

Table 2-1 compares the basic features of these options.

Banks, Savings and Loans, and Credit Unions – which we'll refer to in this discussion as just *banks* – offer Savings Accounts, Money Market Accounts, and Certificates of Deposit (CDs).

Table 2-1

Comparison of U.S. Savings Bonds with other low-risk investments

	Safe from borrower default	Safe from capital loss	Safe from inflation	Rates	Redemption limits	No fee	Tax advantages
Bank Savings Accounts	FDIC or equivalent insurance to $100,000 per account	Yes	No	Adjustable	No	Yes	No
Bank Money Market Accounts							
Bank Certificates of Deposit				Fixed	Early withdrawal penalty		
Money Market Mutual Funds	Minimal risk			Adjustable	No	No	
Bond Mutual Funds	Depends on fund	No	TIPS funds only	Fixed			
Insurance Policies and Annuities	Depends on policy	Yes	Depends on policy	Depends on policy	Yes		Yes
Marketable Treasury Securities	Guaranteed by the US Government	No	Yes, with TIPS	Fixed	No with commission	Only when bought at auction	No
Series EE Savings Bonds		Yes	No	Fixed	1-year limit	Yes	Yes
Series I Savings Bonds			Yes	Fixed base-rate plus inflation adjustment	Early redemption penalty		

Mutual fund companies offer Money Market Funds and various types of bond funds, only some of which are low-risk.

Insurance companies offer life-insurance policies and annuities that offer low-risk at a high price.

In addition to Savings Bonds, the U.S. Treasury offers marketable Treasury Securities, such as T-Bills, T-Notes, and Treasury Inflation Protected Securities, or TIPS.

Safety – default, capital loss, inflation

Safety is the defining characteristic of low-risk investments. If an investment isn't safe, it isn't low-risk. There are several dimensions on which you can measure the safety of an investment.

Safe from borrower default refers to the possibility that the institution you've loaned your money to won't be able to pay you back.

★ Treasury securities, including Savings Bonds, are guaranteed by the Federal government, which is as safe as you can get

★ Bank products have government insurance up to $100,000 per account, which is the next level of safety.

★ Money market mutual funds aren't insured, but are considered to be at the next level of safety because they invest on very short terms

★ The safety of corporate bonds, bond mutual funds, and insurance products depends entirely on the company and the product and varies widely

Safe from capital loss refers to the possibility that the value of your investment could drop below what you paid for it.

The value of traditional corporate and government bonds and bond mutual funds drops as interest rates rise. The effect is minimal in short term funds but exaggerated in long term funds.

For example, if a bond's maturity is 20 years away, its value drops roughly 12 percent for each 1 percentage point rise in the prevailing level of interest rates being paid for similar bonds.

Safe from inflation refers to the possibility that the value of your investment could melt away because of inflation. We'll discuss this in detail in Chapter 3.

Series I Savings Bonds offer inflation protection, as do Treasury Inflation Protected Securities (TIPS). TIPS are the Treasury's big-boy version of Series I bonds. The rules for TIPS, however, are different from the rules for I bonds. Among other differences, TIPS carry the risk of capital loss.

Fixed-rate investments, on the other hand, including Series EE bonds, standard government and corporate bonds, and bank certificates of deposit, have no inflation protection. Severe inflation would reduce the value of these investments with no hope of recovery.

Rates

Typically bank savings accounts and money market funds offer the lowest rates. However, these rates aren't locked in. They adjust up or down with the prevailing level of interest rates.

Bank CDs, on the other hand, lock you into today's rate. They come in a variety of terms – typically the longer you're willing to take today's rate, the higher that rate will be.

You can also get higher rates by investing more. Jumbo CDs, which usually have a minimum investment of $100,000, have higher rates than CDs with a $1,000 minimum.

If you're interested in what rates are being offered right now by banks on their accounts and CDs, go to our web site, click on Book Notes, and see Note 2-3.

To see today's market rates for passbook savings, money market accounts, and a variety of CD terms and sizes, go to our web site, click on Book Notes, then on Note 2-3.

Redemption Limits

The ease with which you can turn your investment into cash is called liquidity. Savings Bonds aren't liquid at all for the first year, they are liquid with a three-month interest penalty after the first year and until five years, and they are totally liquid after that.

* ★ Bank savings accounts and bank and mutual fund money market accounts are the most liquid low-risk investment, but they also pay the lowest rates
* ★ Bank certificates of deposit, like Savings Bonds, have early redemption penalties
* ★ Insurance products are typically not liquid for many years and even then have significant withdrawal penalties
* ★ Marketable Treasury securities are liquid, but you will have to pay a commission to a security broker to handle the sales transaction for you.
* ★ The liquidity of other corporate and government bonds varies, although bond mutual funds are very liquid

Sales and management fees

Sales and management fees are a huge drawback to insurance products. All mutual funds have management fees. Buying and selling mutual funds and marketable Treasury securities can involve broker's commissions, although if you buy directly from the mutual fund company or using TreasuryDirect you can avoid those.

Tax advantages

Traditional IRAs, retirement accounts such as 401Ks, and insurance products have tax advantages that are somewhat like Savings Bonds – you don't pay tax on your earnings until you withdraw your money.

However an important difference is that income tax on your *initial investment* is also deferred with retirement accounts, while with Savings Bonds it's not.

With Savings Bonds you pay tax only on the *interest* you've earned; with traditional retirement accounts you pay tax on your *total withdrawal*.

Roth IRAs have the best tax advantages – you don't pay any tax at all on the money you earn.

Municipal bonds and bond funds are free of federal income tax. Federal securities are free of state and local income tax. There are some money market mutual funds that invest in municipal bonds of a single state that are totally free of federal, state, and city taxes for residents of that state.

Summary: low-risk investment options

Savings Bonds have some similar features with other low-risk investment options, but offer:

* ★ very low risk
* ★ deferral of federal income taxes
* ★ exemption from state income taxes
* ★ flexible redemption term of 1 to 30 years with no risk of capital loss
* ★ inflation protection (Series I only)

Although these features are more valuable to some people than to others, they do have value. Because of that value, Savings Bonds should have a lower interest rate than the other options. When they have the same or a higher rate, Savings Bonds are definitely the better deal.

When Savings Bond rates are lower than other investment options, each individual investor has to determine how valuable the features of Savings Bonds are in his or her situation and make the choice.

This book is designed to help you determine the value of these features in your situation so you can make an informed choice.

What's a marketable Treasury security?

In this chapter we've mentioned marketable Treasury securities several times. Let's take a quick look and make sure we all know what these are.

In addition to Savings Bonds, the U.S. Treasury sells investors Treasury Bills (T-Bills), Treasury Notes (T-Notes), Treasury Bonds (T-Bonds), and Treasury Inflation Protected Securities (TIPS).

If you have a TreasuryDirect account (see Chapter 6), you can use it to buy these securities as well as Savings Bonds.

Because T-Bills, T-Notes, T-Bonds, and TIPS can all be bought and sold in the open market after they are issued, as a group they are known as marketable Treasury securities.

Table 2-2

Savings Bonds versus marketable Treasury securities

Feature	Savings Bonds	Marketable Treasury Securities
Form	Paper (definitive) or Electronic (book)	Electronic only
Minimum Investment	$25	$1,000
Increments above Minimum	Paper – $25 Electronic – $0.01	$1,000 increments only
Maximum Annual Investment	$30,000 per series per type per year	No limit
When can you invest?	Any business day	TreasuryDirect: A few specific days a year Broker: Any business day (fee)
When can you redeem?	Any business day after 1 year	Any business day (fee)
Systematic Investments?	Yes, several types	No
Capital gains and losses?	No	Yes
Interest compounds?	Series EE, Series I – Yes Series H, Series HH – No	No
Income tax on interest earnings can be deferred?	Yes	No
Exempt from state and local income tax?	Yes	Yes
Maturities	30 years; can be redeemed after 1 year; 3-month interest penalty when redeemed before 5 years; never a redemption fee	2, 3, 5, 10, 20, and less than 1 year maturities; can be purchased using TreasuryDirect and held to maturity or redeemed early using Sell Direct ($45 fee)
Inflation protection?	Yes, with Series I	Yes, with TIPS

As you can tell by scanning Table 2-2, marketable Treasury securities are the professional version of Savings Bonds. The minimum and maximum investment levels are very different,

Like Savings Bonds, marketable Treasury securities are backed by the full faith and credit of the U.S. government and are exempt from state and local income taxes.

Compared to Savings Bonds, marketable Treasury securities usually earn higher rates and have the potential for capital gains and losses.

To buy marketable Treasury securities in the open market rather than directly from the Treasury using TreasuryDirect, you would contact a broker, who will charge you a commission.

The Treasury securities sold by brokers aren't new issues, but previously-issued securities. TreasuryDirect customers are limited to investments in newly-issued securities, which are only available on specific days. With Savings Bonds, on the other hand, you can invest on any business day.

Because marketable Treasury securities are only issued on certain dates, if you place an order using your TreasuryDirect account, the transaction will happen on the next date the security you want is available.

Securities you buy through TreasuryDirect can be redeemed on any business day using a TreasuryDirect feature called *Sell Direct*, which has a $45 fee. If you hold your securities until final maturity there's no redemption fee.

Compared to marketable Treasury securities, Savings Bonds have several features that are advantageous for individual investors. They support systematic investing and compounding of interest, are tax deferred, and can be purchased and redeemed at any time (after one year) without a fee or commission.

Types of marketable Treasury securities

Treasury Bills have a maturity of one year or less. They typically mature in 4-, 13- or 26-weeks. Because Savings Bonds have to be held one year before they can be redeemed, they don't compete with short-term T-Bills.

T-Bills are usually available for purchase on the following schedule:

* ★ 13- and 26-week bills – Mondays
* ★ 4-week bills – Tuesdays

Treasury Notes (T-Notes) are issued in 2-, 3-, 5-, and 10-year maturities. The Treasury uses the current rate on the 10-year T-Note to help determine where it should set the Series EE rate. The Treasury also issues a 30-year Treasury Bond (T-Bond).

T-Notes and T-Bonds are available for purchase on the following schedule:

* ★ 2-year – at the end of every month
* ★ 3-year – mid-month in Feb, May, Aug, and Nov
* ★ 5-year – mid-month of every month
* ★ 10-year – mid month in Feb, Mar, May, Jun, Aug, Sep, Nov, and Dec
* ★ 30-year – mid-month in Feb and Aug

Treasury Inflation Protected Securities – The Treasury issues these in 5-, 10-, and 20-year maturities. Like Series I Savings Bonds, they have a fixed base-rate of interest that doesn't change during the life of the security.

Unlike Series I Savings Bonds, however, the fixed portion of a TIPS interest payment isn't added to the value of the security, but is paid to you every six months.

The inflation adjustment portion of TIPS, on the other hand, is added to the TIPS principal amount each month. This is similar to a Series I bond, but with I bonds, the principal amount is adjusted through the inflation component of the interest rate.

When deflation occurs, the TIPS principal amount goes down. With Series I Savings Bond, deflation adjustments are limited to zeroing out the fixed base-rate. There is basically no limit to the size of the TIPS deflation adjustment, which gives an advantage to Savings Bonds. However, if you hold a TIPS until it matures, the Treasury does guarantee that at a minimum you'll get your original investment back.

Another advantage to Series I bonds is that there's no risk of capital loss. When the level of the TIPS base rate goes up, the market value of a TIPS goes down.

The ratio is about 4% of value per 1% of interest rate change for TIPS 5 years from maturity, 8% of value per 1% change for TIPS 10 years from maturity, and 12% of value per 1% change for TIPS 20 years from maturity.

The value of a Savings Bond investment does not change with interest rate changes, meaning you don't risk capital loss if interest rates rise and you don't benefit from capital gains if interest rates decline. In fact, if rates rise you can cash in your low-rate I bonds and purchase new bonds with a higher fixed base-rate.

Neither TIPS nor Savings Bonds are callable. This means the Treasury can't just give you your money back before final maturity, which it would be tempted to do with severe inflation.

Finally, TIPS don't have the deferred-tax feature of Savings Bonds. Moreover, you have to pay income tax each year not only on the interest you receive, but also on the inflation adjustments – and you don't see any cash from the inflation adjustments until the security matures. You can remedy this by holding TIPS in a tax-deferred account, like an IRA or 401K fund, but then you lose their state and local income tax exemption.

Unless a large difference develops between their fixed base-rates, Series I Savings Bonds are always the better choice for individual investors.

To make a comparison based on today's rates, go to our web site and click on Book Notes. Note 2-4 will show you the current Series I fixed rate and note 2-5 will link you to the current open-market rates for TIPS at 5, 7, and 10-year maturities.

TIPS are available for purchase on the following schedule:
- ★ 5-year – end of April and October
- ★ 10-year – mid-month in January, April, July, and October
- ★ 20-year – end of January and July.

Treasury-based funds

It's also possible to invest in marketable Treasury securities through mutual funds and exchange traded funds. For mutual funds, take a look at the offerings from Vanguard. For exchange traded funds, look at the offerings from iShares. Book Note 2-6 links to their web sites.

If you're interested in investigating marketable Treasury securities further, see the following links on our web site. Click on Book Notes, then on the note shown here:

2-7 – Open a TreasuryDirect account for marketable Treasury securities.

2-8 – The U.S. Treasury's web site for T-Bills, T-Notes, and TIPS.

2-9 – Tentative schedule of upcoming Treasury auctions.

Risks of Savings Bonds

Although Savings Bonds have few risks, they aren't entirely riskless. However, their largest risk is one that may surprise you.

Over 5% of the Savings Bonds outstanding have stopped earning interest. This means that the largest risk you face with an investment in Savings Bonds is that you'll forget you have them, or that you'll die and your heirs won't find them.

If you're going to invest in Savings Bonds, you need to make sure this doesn't happen to you.

In Chapter 13, we'll give you some additional information about how to find out if you - or those who have left you an inheritance - own forgotten Savings Bonds.

We'll also give you additional information in Chapter 9 about how to keep track of the Savings Bonds you own, and how to make sure your heirs know you have them.

The only other significant risk of Savings Bonds concerns the electronic bonds at TreasuryDirect. If someone obtains the password to your account, they effectively have control of your money. And the Treasury will not cover any losses.

Finally, as we mentioned earlier, while the registration feature of Savings Bonds keeps others from cashing your bonds, banks sometimes make mistakes. It's best to keep your paper Savings Bonds where thieves can't find them and your heirs can't miss them.

Chapter 3

Today's choices – Series I and Series EE

Historical overview of inflation and interest rates

Series I Savings Bonds feature inflation protection

Series EE Savings Bonds feature fixed rates

Series I versus Series EE

Historical overview of inflation and interest rates

Savings Bonds earn interest. As a Savings Bond investor, you will find it helpful to know about the historical swings in the levels of inflation and interest rates.

The primary force that moves interest rates up and down is inflation. We'll begin this section by looking at inflation, followed by interest rate levels, and we'll finish up by looking at *real interest rates* – the interest rate after removing inflation.

A long-term look at inflation

One of the longest series of economic statistics available today is the Consumer Price Index, for which we have over 200 years of data.

The Consumer Price Index is a measure of *inflation* and *deflation* – a general increase or decrease in the price of goods and services. During times of inflation, a dollar loses value, as it buys less and less. During times of deflation, on the other hand, it buys more and more.

The line in Figure 3-1 shows the annual percent change in the index. As you can see, prices have been quite volatile historically. However, periods of what television pundits like to call "skyrocketing" inflation have usually been associated with wars.

The vertical bars in Figures 3-1, 3-2, and 3-3 highlight the years 1812-1814 (War of 1812), 1861-1865 (Civil War), 1914-1919 (World War I), 1941-1945 (World War II), 1950-1953 (Korean War), 1965-1974 (Vietnam War), 1991 (Gulf War) and 2003-present (Iraq War).

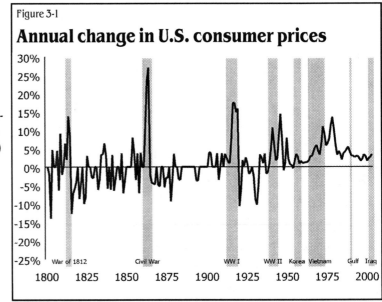

Figure 3-1

Annual change in U.S. consumer prices

As you can see, it is highly unusual for inflation rates to exceed 5 percent, except during wars. During the half-century between 1865 and 1915, inflation did not exceed 4 percent even once (1898's 10-week-long Spanish-American War notwithstanding).

Is inflation good or bad?

Investors and those who have lent money to others hate inflation. It means the dollars they get back when they are repaid aren't worth as much as the dollars they invested or loaned out. That's why interest rates go up with the inflation rate.

On the other hand, borrowers who have fixed-rate loans, such as home mortgages, love inflation, since they can pay back their loans with cheaper dollars. Whether inflation is good or bad depends on your perspective.

A long-term look at interest rates

Historical data on interest rates isn't available as far back as price data, but by combing two data series on high-quality corporate bonds, we can get back as far as 1857. Figure 3-2 overlays this average annual long-term interest rate data on top of the graph in Figure 3-1.

Compared to the jittery line showing the annual change in consumer prices, interest rates change slowly. During the 89-year stretch from 1879 to 1967, these rates were consistently below six percent.

Perhaps the major lesson of Figure 3-2 is that although the "skyrocketing inflation" of the late 1970s was nothing new, the "skyrocketing inter-

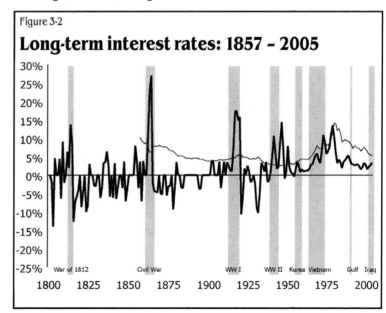

Figure 3-2

Long-term interest rates: 1857 – 2005

est rates" that followed were something we hadn't experienced since before the Civil War.

For the last 35 years, interest rates have followed the inflation rate. In earlier years this didn't happen. I think this is because information about the inflation rate is more widely available and understood now than before, but I'm a journalist. Economists have different theories.

Inflation and real interest rates

Now consider this. Investors who earn six percent interest in a year in which the inflation rate is six percent actually earn nothing at all. The interest payments they receive merely make their principal, which inflation has dwindled, whole again.

Likewise, borrowers who pay six percent interest in a year when the inflation rate is six percent actually pay no interest at all.

And borrowers who pay six percent interest in a year when the inflation rate is nine percent actually earn three percent interest on the amount they've borrowed! (At these rates investors lose three percent of their investment to inflation.)

When you subtract the inflation rate from the interest rate, the result is what is known as the *real interest rate*.

Figure 3-3 keeps the thin interest rate line from Figure 3-2, but instead of the inflation rate, its thick line shows the real interest rate in the U.S. since 1871.

You might remember my earlier observation about inflation being associated with wars. Since high inflation causes low real interest rates, we again can see the Civil War, World War I, World War II, and the end of the Vietnam war,

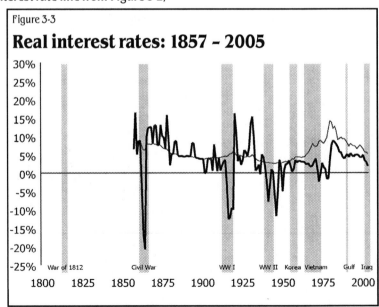

Figure 3-3

Real interest rates: 1857 – 2005

but now they show up as the real interest rate dropping under the zero line of Figure 3-3.

During these times investors earned less than the inflation rate and were losing money.

When real interest rates are below zero, investors are suffering and borrowers are getting rich. Wars tend to be bad times for investors and good times for borrowers.

What causes inflation?

Economists attribute inflation to "too much money chasing too few goods." The amount of money in circulation is controlled by a country's central bank – in the case of the U.S. that's the Federal Reserve.

There's no need to go into the details of how it all works here, it's just important to understand that inflation isn't random but starts with the actions of the Federal Reserve.

At the same time, you have to recognize that the controls that the Federal Reserve has to steer inflation don't work like a rudder. It's more like paddling a canoe with your spouse in the back and the kids fighting in the middle than piloting a cabin cruiser.

Given all that, what we want to know as investors is where the Federal Reserve will try to dock inflation in the years ahead.

It seems like a simple answer to me. Just remember that borrowers love inflation and the that U.S. is in debt in every imaginable way – government debt, trade debt, and personal debt.

At a time when the government should be running budget surpluses to save up for the future expense of Medicare and Social Security, it's running ever-larger deficits. Personal debt and trade debt are totally out of control.

Where will the money come from to pay back these debts? Politically speaking, it's a lot easier to let the inflation rate go up a percentage point or two than it is to raise the equivalent amount by reducing benefits or by raising taxes.

Hang on to your life jackets.

Book Note 3-1 links to an article about a report written by Standard & Poors, a company that rates bonds for investors. The report poses a scenario in which central banks allow inflation to reach 20% annually to control government debt caused by aging populations.

Series I Savings Bonds feature inflation protection

Series I Savings Bonds have been issued since September 1998. In addition to the basic features mentioned in Chapter 1:

★ Series I bonds earn a composite of a fixed base-rate, which is set for the life of the bond at issue, and the current inflation rate, which is updated every six months.

- ★ There's no announced formula for setting the fixed base-rate component. As shown in Table 3-1, this component has ranged from a low of 1.0% to a high of 3.60%.

- ★ The Treasury uses the *Consumer Price Index for All Urban Consumers*, (CPI-U) published by the Bureau of Labor Statistics, to determine the I bond inflation rate component. Since I bonds were introduced in September 1998, the annual rate of the inflation component has ranged from a low of 0.56% to a high of 5.70%. Historical inflation components are shown in Table 3-2.

- ★ In the event that the inflation rate is negative, it's possible for the inflation component to cancel out all or part of the fixed rate component. However, the Treasury has guaranteed that the composite rate will never go below zero.

I bond fixed base-rates

Use Table 3-1 to determine the exact fixed base-rate for your Series I Savings Bonds.

The Treasury sets the Series I Savings Bond fixed base-rate administratively, which means the criteria it uses aren't public information and the rate can't be predicted in advance.

New fixed base-rates are announced at the beginning of May and November each year and apply to new Savings Bonds issued during the following six-month period. Once an I bond is issued, however, its fixed base-rate never changes.

Table 3-1

Series I bond fixed base-rate component

Issue date	Fixed base-rate	Issue date	Fixed base-rate
Sep 98 – Oct 98	3.40%	Nov 98 – Apr 99	3.30%
May 99 – Oct 99	3.30%	Nov 99 – Apr 00	3.40%
May 00 – Oct 00	3.60%	Nov 00 – Apr 01	3.40%
May 01 – Oct 01	3.00%	Nov 01 – Apr 02	2.00%
May 02 – Oct 02	2.00%	Nov 02 – Apr 04	1.60%
May 03 – Oct 03	1.10%	Nov 03 – Apr 04	1.10%
May 04 – Oct 04	1.00%	Nov 04 – Apr 05	1.00%
May 05 – Oct 05	1.20%	Nov 05 – Apr 06	1.00%
May 06 – Oct 06	1.40%	Nov 06 – Apr 07	1.40%
May 07 – Oct 07		Nov 07 – Apr 08	
May 08 – Oct 08		Nov 08 – Apr 09	

Figure 3-4 shows the information in Table 3-1 graphically. In addition, it overlays rates for TIPS, the Treasury's other inflation-protected security, which is traded in the open market.

Because they are traded, the rates of TIPS change daily. The Federal Reserve publishes daily data on TIPS interest rates. This data goes back to January 2, 2003 for 5-year and 10-year TIPS, and to July 27, 2004 for 20-year TIPS. Each Friday's figure is shown as a data point in Figure 3-4.

For data before 2003, Figure 3-4 shows the yield of each TIPS on the day it was issued. This data series is a mix of 5, 10, and 30-year TIPS.

If the I bond fixed base-rate goes up in the future, there's nothing preventing you from cashing in I bonds with a low rate and buying new ones. See the section on *Savings Bond rollovers* in Chapter 14 for additional information.

You'll find an updated, easy-to-read color version of Figure 3-4 on our web site. See Book Note 3-2. The same page includes the data you need to update Table 3-1.

A link to the Federal Reserve's interest rate data is at Book Note 3-3.

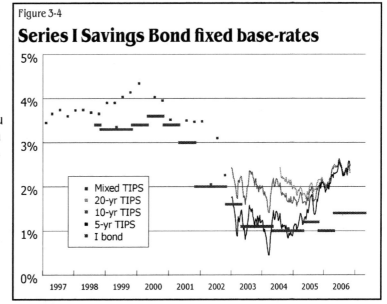

Figure 3-4

Series I Savings Bond fixed base-rates

Legend:
- Mixed TIPS
- 20-yr TIPS
- 10-yr TIPS
- 5-yr TIPS
- I bond

Series I bond inflation component

Table 3-2 shows the historical inflation rate components for each rate period since I bonds were introduced.

Table 3-2

Series I bond inflation component

Rate period beginning	Inflation component	Rate period beginning	Inflation component
Sep 98 — Oct 98	1.24%	Nov 98 — Apr 99	1.73%
May 99 — Oct 99	1.71%	Nov 99 — Apr 00	3.52%
May 00 — Oct 00	3.81%	Nov 00 — Apr 01	3.04%
May 01 — Oct 01	2.88%	Nov 01 — Apr 02	2.38%
May 02 — Oct 02	0.56%	Nov 02 — Apr 04	2.46%
May 03 — Oct 03	3.54%	Nov 03 — Apr 04	1.09%
May 04 — Oct 04	2.38%	Nov 04 — Apr 05	2.66%
May 05 — Oct 05	3.58%	Nov 05 — Apr 06	5.69%
May 06 — Oct 06	1.00%	Nov 06 — Apr 07	3.10%
May 07 — Oct 07		Nov 07 — Apr 08	
May 08 — Oct 08		Nov 08 — Apr 09	

Book Note 3-4 links to a page with the data you need to update Table 3-2.

The climbing line in Figure 3-5 shows the level of the CPI-U for each month since Series I bonds were introduced. The CPI-U uses the price levels of 1982-1984 as its base of 100.

The horizontal lines in the graph are each six-months long and begin on their left end in March or September and end on their right end the following September or March.

The up-and-down space between these lines represents the change in the CPI-U during the six-month period.

The percentages on the graph indicate the change, expressed as an annual rate, for each six-month period. These are the same percentages the Treasury uses to calculate composite Series I bond interest rates.

Since I bonds were introduced in 1998, the I bond inflation component has never gone negative, but it has come close. In September 2001 the index set a high for that year and then started to decline. By March the index had barely made it back above the September level. The same thing happened again in September 2005.

If the inflation component goes negative, it can lower or even wipe out an I bond's fixed rate. However, an I bond's composite rate can't go below zero, no matter how deeply the CPI-U dips. This gives I bonds an advantage over the Treasury's big-boy inflation security, TIPS, which do decline in value when the CPI-U change is negative.

Series I bond composite rate

For each rate period, an I bond's composite rate is the sum of:
★ the bond's fixed base-rate
★ the annualized inflation rate
★ an inflation adjustment to the fixed base-rate (the fixed rate times one-half the annualized inflation rate)

Figure 3-5 is updated monthly on our web site. It's at Book Note 3-4.

The third item, the inflation adjustment to the fixed base-rate, adds just a few hundredths of a percent to the composite rate, but always makes the composite rate higher than you'd expect it to be from adding together the fixed base-rate and the inflation rate.

For example, an I bond fixed-base rate of 1.40% and an inflation component of 1.00%, creates a composite rate of 2.41%, not the 2.40% you would reasonably expect.

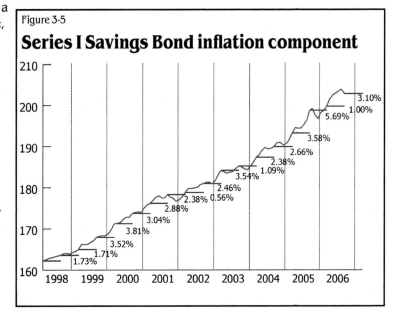

Figure 3-5

Series I Savings Bond inflation component

Series EE Savings Bonds feature fixed rates

Series EE Savings Bonds were first issued in January 1980. The rules governing these bonds have changed several times, most recently in May 2005. Each bond follows the rules in effect when it was issued, so how interest rates are calculated for any specific bond depends on its issue date.

The May 2005 rule change was significant. Series EE bonds issued before May 2005 earn interest rates that are adjusted every six months. Now Series EE bonds earn a fixed rate of interest.

We'll discuss the rules for older series EE and E bonds in Chapter 7. In addition to the basic features mentioned in Chapter 1, the rules for today's Series EE bonds are:

★ The interest rate is fixed at the time of issue and will not change during the bond's original maturity period, which lasts 20 years. The Treasury reserves the right to change the rate at that time. The new rate would be good for the bond's final ten years.

★ The fixed rate is based on the 10-year Treasury Note yield during the six months before rates are set, but there's no specific formula for setting the rate.

★ Paper Series EE bonds are sold at half face value. You pay $50 for a $100 Savings Bond. As mentioned earlier, this marketing gimmick has caused Savings Bonds owners, winners, and gift recipients waves of confusion. Electronic EE bonds and both paper and electronic I bonds don't have this feature.

★ Tied to the half-face-value gimmick, Series EE bonds have an *original maturity guarantee* (see Chapter 7) that promises they will double in value during their original 20-year maturity period. This guarantee is meaningless when the fixed rate is 3.5% or more. Those bonds will double in value in less than 20 years.

Table 3-3 shows the fixed rates of Savings Bonds issued since May 2005.

Table 3-3 **Series EE bond fixed rates**		
Issue date	**Fixed rate**	**Reaches face value in**
May 05 – Oct 05	3.50%	20 years
Nov 05 – Apr 06	3.20%	20 years
May 06 – Oct 06	3.70%	18 years, 11 months
Nov 06 – Apr 07	3.60%	19 years, 5 months
May 07 – Oct 07		
Nov 07 – Apr 08		
May 08 – Oct 08		
Nov 08 – Apr 09		

Book Note 3-5 links to the page on our web site that has the data you need to update Table 3-3

Series I versus Series EE

So which one is the better investment, Series I or Series EE? My advice? Right now, I like the I.

The arguments against the I bond

Let's begin, however, by looking at the two primary objections investors have to the Series I bond – its low fixed base-rate and taxes on inflation.

The I bond's low fixed base-rate

The first objection most people have to the I bond is its low fixed rate. This thinking goes something like this , "I can't hit my investment goals with a growth rate that low. I have to have an investment that pays more."

If you find yourself going down this line of thinking, my caution to you is to remember:

★ Don't be fooled by randomness. The probability of losing even part of the money you invest in riskier ventures outweighs the potential benefit of larger returns. Series I bonds guarantee that your money won't be diminished, not even by inflation. ***No other investment comes with this guarantee.***

★ Earning just the I bond fixed rate and inflation seems meager, but what are your options? Subtract the I bond fixed rate from the EE bond's fixed rate. If you invest in the EE instead of the I bond, you're saying you expect inflation to be less than that while you hold the bond. As we'll see in a few pages, such a low inflation rate is unlikely.

What you have to remember is that although other investments don't have an inflation component, inflation is still eating away their returns. The Series I bond protects you from this, so its base rate is lower. If you can't earn more, after inflation, with an alternative investment, then even the low I bond fixed base-rate is the best rate going.

Paying income tax on inflation

In his 1999 book, *Savings Bonds: When to Hold, When to Fold and Everything In-Between*, Dan Pederson of the Savings Bond Informer, asked, "Hey, where's the protection?"

Pederson rightly points out that since you have to pay income tax on I bond interest, and I bond interest includes an inflation component, I bond owners end up paying income tax on inflation.

Pederson is correct, but just because alternative investments don't have a specific inflation component doesn't mean you're not paying tax on inflation. Other investments just include your payback for inflation in the base rate. Or at least you hope they do!

The logical end to Pederson's argument is to put your money in the mattress and earn 0.00%. That way you'll never have to worry about paying taxes on inflation. But you'll be worse off.

There are some investments in which inflation creates capital gains (a price increase on something you own) rather than ordinary income (interest or dividends).

Capital gains are taxed at a lower rate for most people. But these investments aren't low-risk. And part of the risk is that the value of the investment won't keep up with inflation – a risk you avoid with I bonds.

The arguments in favor of the I bond

There are three reasons I like Series I bonds today over Series EE – historical results, inflation projections, and the choices other investors are making.

Historical results

Table 3-4 shows the actual result you would have received had you purchased both an EE bond and an I bond every month since I bonds were introduced in September 1998.

Table 3-4

Series I versus Series EE results
(as of end of rate periods that begin November 2006 through April 2007)

Issue Date	Series EE redemption value per $100 invested	Series I redemption value per $100 invested	Series I to EE difference	Series I fixed base-rate
Sep 98 – Oct 98	$141.52	$166.76	17.84%	3.40%
Nov 98 – Apr 99	$139.92	$165.36	18.18%	3.30%
May 99 – Oct 99	$136.96	$161.20	17.70%	3.30%
Nov 99 – Apr 00	$133.92	$158.36	18.25%	3.40%
May 00 – Oct 00	$130.72	$155.16	18.70%	3.60%
Nov 00 – Apr 01	$126.88	$147.64	16.36%	3.40%
May 01 – Oct 01	$123.52	$139.68	13.08%	3.00%
Nov 01 – Apr 02	$120.72	$128.44	6.40%	2.00%
May 02 – Oct 02	$118.40	$125.68	6.15%	2.00%
Nov 02 – Apr 03	$114.96	$120.48	4.80%	1.60%
May 03 – Oct 03	$113.04	$115.92	2.55%	1.10%
Nov 03 – Apr 04	$111.52	$113.24	1.54%	1.10%
May 04 – Oct 04	$110.16	$111.76	1.45%	1.00%
Nov 04 – Apr 05	$108.56	$109.92	1.25%	1.00%
May 05 – Oct 05	$106.24	$108.28	1.92%	1.20%
Nov 05 – Apr 06	$104.00	$105.48	1.42%	1.00%
May 06 – Oct 06	$102.80	$102.32	-0.47%	1.40%
Nov 06 – Apr 07	$100.88	$101.12	0.24%	1.40%

The second and third columns of Table 3-4 show the redemption value, per $100 invested, of all these bonds. The value is calculated as of the end of the rate periods that begin November 2006 through April 2007.

The fourth column shows that except for purchases during the six-month May – October 2006 period, I bonds have **always** been the better investment. The early I bonds, in particular, have earned over 10% more than EE bonds issued the same month.

Nonetheless, the degree to which I bonds are the better investment has become less and less as their fixed base-rates, which are shown in the final column, have declined.

In all but the bottom four lines of Table 3-4, the Series EE bonds have adjustable-rates. These older adjustable-rate bonds may be able to overtake I bonds if interest rates go up and inflation goes down. But the probability of that particular combination of events is pretty low.

The probability of the May-October 2006 I bonds outperforming the equivalent EE bonds in the future, on the other hand, is pretty good.

Inflation projections

There's another way to look at the choice today's Savings Bond investors have. To decide which is better, look at the difference between the Series EE rate and the I bond's fixed base-rate. For example, if the EE bond rate is 3.50% and the fixed-rate portion of the Series I rate is 1.0%, that's a difference of 2.50 percentage points.

If inflation is higher than this difference during the period you hold the bond, the Series I bonds will earn more. If inflation is less, Series EE bonds will earn more.

Since no one can predict the future, no one can tell you for sure which Series is the better choice. However, the history of inflation does give us some probabilities.

Earlier in this chapter we looked at long-term inflation rates. Now we're going to look at the same data in a slightly different way.

The exact Consumer Price Index data that the Treasury uses to determine the I bond inflation component is available going back 93 years to 1913. Figure 3-6 shows what the I bond inflation component would have been had I bonds been available during this entire period.

If you compare this data the to the comparable data in Figure 3-1, one difference you'll notice is that the large deflationary dips in Figure 3-1 stop at just under 0% in this figure.

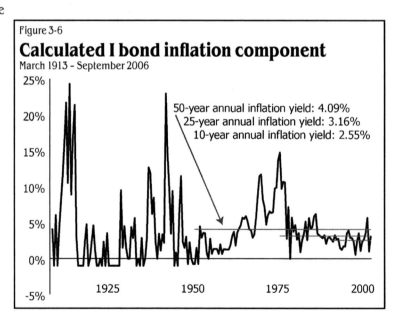

Figure 3-6

Calculated I bond inflation component

March 1913 – September 2006

50-year annual inflation yield: 4.09%
25-year annual inflation yield: 3.16%
10-year annual inflation yield: 2.55%

That's because of the way the I bond rate is set in deflationary times. A negative inflation component can wipe out an I bond's fixed base-rate, but it can't go lower than that.

The three horizontal lines at the right side of Figure 3-6 show you the annual yield of the I Bond inflation component over the last 50, 25, and 10 years.

Because of the deflationary dips in the early part of the 20th century, the inflation yield for the entire 93.5-year period depends on how low you allow the I Bond to dip with inflation.

If you use the highest fixed base-rate I bonds have ever had, 3.60%, the inflation yield for the entire period would be 3.66%.

On the other hand, if you take the new Federal Reserve chairman at his word that he would take any measure ("drop money out of helicopters" was his vivid expression) to prevent deflation in the future and you use 0.00%, the inflation yield for the entire period would be 4.07%.

So, in any case, the inflation yield for the entire period is somewhere between the 25-year and 50-year lines.

When the difference between the Series EE fixed rate and the I bond's fixed base-rate is 2.50 percentage points, inflation during the period you hold your bond would have to dip below even the low average of the last ten years to make the Series EE bond the better investment.

On the other hand, if inflation hugs the level it's been at the last ten years, you'll do better with the I bond.

And if inflation looks more like it has over the last 25 to 50 years during the period you hold the bond, the I bond's inflation component yield will make I bonds by far the better investment.

Now let's look at the Series EE versus Series I choice in an entirely different way.

Collective Genius

James Surowiecki's book, *The Wisdom of Crowds*, develops the theory of unconscious collective intelligence. It holds that the average decision of large groups of people acting independently is usually the right one.

For more information on The Wisdom of Crowds, see Book Note 3-6.

If you think this theory might work, then you'd like to see some data on how others view the Series I or EE question.

On the left side of Figure 3-7, you can see the annual fiscal year (Oct-Sep) investments in Series EE and I Savings Bonds since Series I bonds were introduced.

For comparison, the right side shows investments during the last six months. These monthly figures have been annualized so that you can easily compare them to the annual figures.

As you can see, Series I bonds have outsold Series EE bonds since FY-2001, although in the summer of 2006 EE bonds were slightly ahead.

I update Figure 3-7 monthly. To see the latest version, go to my web site, click on Book Note 3-7.

During this period the composite I bond rate was a low 2.41% and the EE bond rate was 3.70%. Market rates for bank certificates of deposit were higher than either of these during this period, consequently the level of investment was quite low for both series.

Since the Treasury changed how it sets Series EE rates in May 2005, Series EE investments have been in decline.

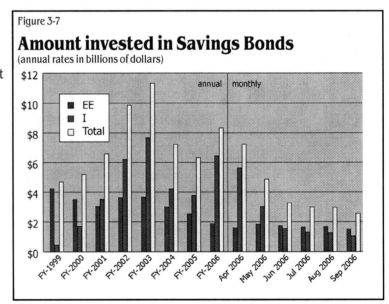

Figure 3-7

Amount invested in Savings Bonds
(annual rates in billions of dollars)

Chapter 4

How to invest in Savings Bonds

The where, who, when, and how much of Savings Bonds

What to expect when you buy paper Savings Bonds

Buying Savings Bonds as gifts

The where, who, when, and how much of Savings Bonds

Where to buy Savings Bonds

The best way to buy Savings Bonds is online. To do this you'll need to open a **TreasuryDirect** account. Electronic bonds can be purchased and redeemed online. Money for the bonds is withdrawn from or deposited into the bank account you specify.

Alternatively, paper Savings Bonds can be purchased and redeemed at more than 40,000 financial institutions in the U.S., probably including your local bank. If you have an online account with your bank, you may also be able to buy paper bonds online through that account.

Systematic Investments

While most Savings Bonds are purchased at financial institutions, many are sold automatically on a scheduled basis, such as every two weeks or every month, through:

★ **TreasuryDirect** – you can set up any schedule you like to buy Savings Bonds and have the funds automatically deducted from your bank account.

★ **TreasuryDirect Deposits** – employers, pension funds, and others can deposit funds into your TreasuryDirect account. For more information, see the section *TreasuryDirect Deposit Option* later in this chapter.

★ **Payroll Savings Plans** – your employer deducts the amount you specify from your paycheck. The deduction can buy paper bonds.

★ **Bond-a-Month Plans** – your bank deducts the amount you specify from your account on whatever schedule you specify.

The Treasury keeps a list of banks that offer Savings Bonds online. Go to our web site, click on Book Notes, and see note 4-1.

Who can buy Savings Bonds?

Anyone who is a resident of the U.S. or its territories and who has a Social Security Number, without regard to citizenship or age, may purchase either electronic or paper Savings Bonds. The same applies to U.S. citizens living abroad. In addition:

★ Civilian employees of the U.S. government and members of its armed forces who have a Social Security Number, as well as residents of Canada or Mexico who work in the U.S. and have a Social Security Number, may buy Savings Bonds through a Payroll Savings Plan.

★ Although you have to have a Social Security Number to *buy* a Savings Bond, any person, without regard to residency, citizenship, or age – with the exception of those living in a few countries restricted by the U.S. Treasury – may be *named in the registration* of a paper Savings Bond. For example, you can buy a gift bond for almost anyone.

★ Paper Savings Bonds of either series may be issued (or re-registered) in the names of fiduciaries such as guardians and similar representatives of minors and others who need help with their financial affairs, as well as in the name of the trustee of a living trust.

★ Paper Series EE bonds may also be registered in the name of a company, organization, association, public body, and additional types of trusts when first issued (but not via re-registration).

★ At this time, electronic bonds at TreasuryDirect can only be registered in the names of individuals with Social Security Numbers

★ Owner, co-owner, beneficiary? See Chapter 5.

For a list of the restricted countries, go to our web site, click on Book Notes, and see note 4-2.

An adult who can't manage his or her affairs may be named as the owner, co-owner or beneficiary of a Savings Bond only if there's been a representative appointed for the estate. If the incompetent person's funds are used to purchase the Savings Bonds, another individual may not be named as co-owner or beneficiary. The Savings Bond registration must include appropriate reference to the guardianship or similar fiduciary arrangement.

When to buy Savings Bonds

No matter when you buy a Savings Bond, you will earn interest from the first day of that month. Consequently, it makes sense to buy your Savings Bonds near the end of the month.

If you are buying paper bonds from a bank, the bond's issue month is determined by the day you complete the transaction at the bank.

If you are buying through TreasuryDirect, on the other hand, the bond's issue month depends on the day the Treasury receives the fund transfer from your bank, so the last day of the month is too late.

How much you can invest

Minimum Investment

Compared to other types of interest-bearing investments, Savings Bonds, which can be purchased for as little as $25, have a very low purchase limit. This makes them suitable for entry-level investors and those who want to invest smaller sums on a scheduled basis.

TreasuryDirect users can buy Series I and EE bonds in any amount, to the penny, from $25 to $30,000.

Paper Series I and EE bonds, on the other hand, are only available with the following face values: $50, $75, $100, $200, $500, $1,000, $5,000, and $10,000.

Maximum Annual Investment

Although Savings Bonds have a low purchase limit, unlike other investments they also have an annual maximum purchase limit of $30,000 per series per type per Social Security Number per year.

For example, in one year you can buy $30,000 worth of I bonds from TreasuryDirect, another $30,000 in paper I bonds. You can do the same with Series EE.

TreasuryDirect will prevent you from going over the limit, but with paper bonds it's possible to invest more than the maximum. Moreover, the Treasury doesn't have a systematic way to check for this with paper bonds. While there's no penalty for going over the limit, if the Treasury discovers your situation, they will refund the part over $30,000 without interest.

You can avoid the limit by having co-owners on your paper bonds and using the co-owner's Social Security Number on each $30,000 set of bonds after your own. As long as the co-owners aren't also investing in Savings Bonds, each SSN will be within its own limits.

TreasuryDirect bonds don't have a denomination or face value. Paper Series I bonds are sold at their full face value; paper EE bonds are sold at one-half their face value – for example, you pay $25 for a $50 paper EE bond.

In all cases you earn interest on the amount you have invested – not on the face value.

What to expect when you buy paper Savings Bonds

In most states, you can buy paper Series I and Series EE Savings Bonds from most banks, credit unions, or savings institutions, even though Savings Bonds aren't a bank product.

However, the bank doesn't hand you the bond on the spot. It helps you fill out a purchase form, takes your money, and gives you a receipt. The banks sends the form and money to a Federal Reserve Bank Savings Bond center, which processes your request and mails the paper bonds to you. It takes about three weeks for the bonds to arrive.

On the form the bank has you fill out, you specify the names for the bond's registration (see Chapter 5), a Social Security Number (either yours or the number of the owner), the bond denominations you want to receive, and the address you'd like the bonds mailed to.

If your bank can't help you, you can also invest in paper Savings Bonds by sending a check directly to the Federal Reserve. Detailed information about how to invest in paper Savings Bonds directly with the Federal Reserve is in the Appendix.

If the Savings Bonds don't arrive

If your bonds don't arrive within 15 business days, contact the institution where you ordered the bonds. They'll work with you and the Federal Reserve to either find the missing bonds or get you replacements.

If you end up signing a form to get a replacement bond, the replacement should be delivered within three weeks.

You can get a copy of the form for claiming Savings Bonds that were never received at Book Note 4-3

If paper bonds you bought through your employer's Payroll Savings Plan don't arrive, work with your payroll office to get them replaced.

Buying Savings Bonds as gifts

Paper Series EE Savings Bonds are often used as gifts. One reason for their popularity is that Series EE bonds are purchased at half of face value. So you can give a Savings Bond that has $100 printed on it, even though its cost to you and its true value is only $50.

When you go to the bank to purchase a Savings Bond, you can make anyone the owner. And, as we saw earlier in this chapter, the recipient of a gift bond can live virtually anywhere in the world.

When you purchase the gift bond, you have to provide a Social Security Number, but it can be either yours or the recipient's.

The Social Security Number you provide isn't used for tax purposes; instead, it's used primarily to track the bond in case it's lost.

Government agencies providing benefits that require the recipient to have limited assets also routinely do a Savings Bond SSN check.

Because of its lost-bond tracking function, it's best to provide the gift recipient's Social Security Number rather than your own. No one ever thinks to look for their lost bond under Aunt Jennifer's SSN.

It's important to understand that when you buy a gift bond, the bank doesn't hand it to you on the spot. The bond will be mailed out by the Treasury and, as we've just discussed, typically takes about three weeks to arrive.

You will also have to provide the mailing address that you'd like the Savings Bond sent to. You can provide your own address or you can have it mailed to the recipient.

If you have it mailed to the recipient, make sure you remember to tell the recipient who the gift came from. When the Savings Bond arrives, there's no way for the recipient to tell who purchased it.

People ask me all the time how to trace the giver of a gift bond, but it can't be done. So you're not going to get a Thank You note from Hannah unless you tell someone about the gift.

Alternatively, you can have the gift Savings Bond mailed to your own address. When you do this, your name and address will be printed in the *mail to* area on the bond.

Joshua can remember you when he cashes it years from now! And you can present it to Joshua in person.

Because of the three-week wait for the bond, which givers sometimes forget to plan for, the Treasury provides banks with certificates that announce the gift, but banks don't always have them at hand.

But you can also customize and download these certificates online – go to our web site and see Book Note 4-4. It links to the Treasury's Savings Bond web site, which has the gift certificates in Adobe Acrobat (.pdf) files.

Savings Bond gift certificates
– Book Note 4-4

You can customize a gift certificate and print it out on your own computer. Unless you have a very slow Internet connection, use the high-resolution files rather than the low-resolution files.

There are different certificates available for birthdays, baby gifts, graduations, weddings, and holidays. There's also a "traditional" version you can customize for other occasions.

Figure 4-1 and 4-2 on the next page use this generic certificate to demonstrate that each .pdf file has two pages. The first page is used to customize the certificate. The second page is the page that you actually print.

Figure 4-1

Filling out the gift certificate

Savings Bond gift certificates – Book Note 4-4

Figure 4-2

Finished Savings Bond gift certificate

Chapter 5

Whose name goes on the bond?

Savings Bond registration issues

A gift is a gift

Registration and estate planning

Possession is 0% of the law

Savings Bond registration issues

The issue that gets the least thought when investors purchase new Savings Bonds is how the bond is registered. First let's look at what the options are, then we'll discuss the pros and cons of the various options.

Owner, co-owner, beneficiary

All Savings Bonds must have a registered owner. The owner's name appears first in the registration. Without documentation showing otherwise – for example, that the co-owner contributed some of the money to buy the bond – the Treasury and the IRS will assume the first-named owner is the *principal owner*, the person who will pay tax income tax on the interest the bond has earned.

★ In TreasuryDirect, the owner must be a person with a Social Security Number

★ Paper Series EE and I bonds also allow the owner to be a fiduciary of certain kinds of trusts, such as a living trust (see Chapter 10) or a trust holding the assets of someone unable to manage his or her financial affairs

★ Paper Series EE bonds, but not I bonds, also allow the owner to be additional types of legal entities and trusts, including companies, organizations, and public bodies

In addition to the owner, a Savings Bond registration can include one other name.

The second registrant can be either a co-owner or a beneficiary. If the registration uses the word WITH (TreasuryDirect) or OR (paper bonds), the second person is the co-owner. If the registration uses the word POD (payable on death), the second person is the beneficiary.

If there is a second registrant, it must be a natural person. It cannot be a legal entity.

For example, a charity can't be a co-owner or beneficiary of your Savings Bonds. However, there's one somewhat self-serving exception to this – you can make the U.S. Treasury your beneficiary.

Three names aren't allowed, so a Savings Bond can't have both a co-owner and a beneficiary.

As discussed in Chapter 6, co-ownership in TreasuryDirect is weaker than co-ownership of a paper bond. The co-owner of a paper bond can cash it without the owner's consent or knowledge, a TreasuryDirect co-owner can't. Likewise, in TreasuryDirect the owner can remove a co-owner without the co-owner's consent or knowledge, but a paper bond owner needs the co-owner's signature for this.

Beneficiaries can cash Savings Bonds only after the owner dies. A death certificate is required as proof that the owner has died.

Unless a Savings Bond owner dies, changing the registered owner almost always creates a taxable event that requires the original owner to declare the interest income up to the date of the registration change.

The exceptions are listed in Chapter 12.

On the other hand, adding, changing, or deleting a co-owner is almost never a taxable event, even though it requires the signature of the co-owner with paper bonds. Older E and H bonds also require the beneficiary's signature to make a change; newer bonds don't require this.

The college education deduction

If you want a Savings Bond to be eligible for the college education deduction, make sure you follow the registration requirements described in Chapter 17. The limitations for this deduction are both many and strict. A mistake in registration could prevent you from getting the deduction.

A gift is a gift

Several times a year I'm asked how the buyer of a bond can cash or change the registration on a gift bond. In these cases the giver and the recipient have had a falling out and the giver wants to take the gift back.

Whoops. Too late. If your name isn't on the bond, you don't have any legal right to the bond, even if you did put up the money. You can't redeem it or change the registration.

However, if you try to avoid this situation by making yourself the co-owner of a gift bond, then the IRS says you owe the tax on the interest income.

Since you put up the money to buy the bond and you have an ownership interest in the bond, you're considered the principal owner, even if you list your name second, after the OR. So when the gift recipient cashes the bond, according to IRS rules, you owe the tax.

Registration and estate planning

There's more information about the role of Savings Bonds in estate planning in Chapter 10, including information on having a Savings Bond issued in the name of a Living Trust.

For now, you need to know that legally, Savings Bond co-owner and beneficiary designations overrule your Last Will and Testament. The funds are available to your heirs immediately, rather than after certification of your Will by a Probate Court, which typically takes six months or more.

This means you can use a Savings Bond's registration to "avoid probate." However, the value of your bonds is still included in your estate for estate tax purposes.

If you want your Will to determine distribution of the proceeds of your Savings Bonds, don't add a co-owner or beneficiary. To summarize:

★   At the death of a registered owner of a Savings Bond, the bond belongs to the co-owner or beneficiary, if the bond has one. If not, the bond becomes part of the owner's estate and is distributed according to the owner's Will, if there is one, or according to state or federal law.

★   If both the registered owner and the co-owner or beneficiary of a Savings Bond die, the bond becomes the property of the estate of the person who died last.

Possession is 0% of the law

Savings Bonds are registered securities. With registered securities, *registration is conclusive of ownership.*

This means that possession of a Savings Bond, or the source of the funds used to buy a Savings Bond, cannot be used to establish ownership.

All that counts is the name in the Treasury's records in West Virginia, which is the same as the name on the bond.

Registration is what prevents Savings Bonds from being marketable – you can't sell a Savings Bond to someone or use it as collateral on a loan because possession of a Savings Bond is meaningless – only those named on the bond itself can redeem it.

Likewise, you can't "give" a bond to your grandchildren or to a charity. Only the owner or co-owner of a bond can redeem it.

Savings Bond fraud

Although non-owners aren't supposed to be able to redeem a Savings Bond, banks handling Savings Bonds have been known to mistakenly redeem them.

Although possession of a Savings Bond is legally meaningless, it's best to keep them where thieves can't find them and your heirs can't miss them.

The Treasury handles issues of fraud on a case-by-case basis. If one or more of your Savings Bonds is redeemed by someone who isn't entitled to it, notify the Treasury using the online method described in the Appendix or by regular mail at:

Savings Bond Operations
Bureau of the Public Debt
P. O. Box 1328
Parkersburg, WV 26106-1328

Chapter 6

All about TreasuryDirect

Paper versus electronic

How to open a new TreasuryDirect account

Using your TreasuryDirect Account

TreasuryDirect payroll savings option

How to convert paper bonds to electronic bonds

Paper versus electronic

Electronic Savings Bonds purchased through TreasuryDirect have these differences compared to paper Savings Bonds.

★ Electronic bonds are safe from fire, floods, and other disasters; you can close that safety deposit box.

★ You can determine the current interest rate and current value of electronic bonds simply by logging in to your TreasuryDirect account .

★ TreasuryDirect transfers money out of or into the bank account you specify – no checks to get lost.

★ Your employer or pension fund can deposit funds in TreasuryDirect as a deduction from your paycheck.

★ You can easily and quickly set up or change systematic investments inside TreasuryDirect.

★ Unlike paper bonds, which have fixed amounts, electronic bonds can be purchased in any amount, to the penny, from $25 to $30,000.

★ Electronic bonds can be partially redeemed. Electronic redemptions must be for at least $25 and the issue month you are cashing in must have a remaining balance of at least $25. Although paper Savings Bonds can also be partially redeemed, it's a hassle and the fixed denominations of paper bonds aren't as flexible.

You can use the TreasuryDirect partial redemption feature to obtain interest payments from Series EE or Series I Savings Bonds. This gives them the **current income feature** that was formerly reserved for Series H and HH Savings Bonds, which are no longer issued.

★ You can transfer your own Savings Bond funds in partial amounts to anyone else who has a TreasuryDirect account. (This will be a taxable event, however.)

★ You can buy electronic Savings Bonds as gifts and either keep them in your account or transfer them to the recipient's account.

★ You can convert paper Savings Bonds to electronic Savings Bonds but you can't convert electronic to paper and you can't buy paper bonds with TreasuryDirect.

★ Electronic bonds can only be registered in the names of individuals who have Social Security Numbers, not trusts or other types of organizations, as with paper bonds.

★ Co-ownership is weaker with electronic bonds. In TreasuryDirect the registration says *account holder* WITH *co-owner*, rather than OR as on paper bonds. The account holder must grant the co-owner view or transact rights before the co-owner can see the bonds in the *Shared Securities* area of their own TreasuryDirect account. This isn't even possible, obviously, unless the co-owner has a TreasuryDirect account. In any case, the owner isn't obligated to grant either kind of right.

★ Moreover, in TreasuryDirect the owner can change or remove a co-owner without the co-owner's knowledge or permission. With paper Savings Bonds the co-owner has to sign the form requesting the change.

★ At redemption, the 1099-INT tax form reporting the interest earned has the Social Security Number of the TreasuryDirect account holder who *purchased* the bond. With EE and I bonds, it's issued in the Social Security Number of the co-owner who *cashed* the bonds. Electronic bonds more closely adhere to IRS regulations.

★ Electronic bonds have no paper trail. If something happens to you, your heirs will have no indication that you own Savings Bonds unless you make that clear in your financial records.

★ In the case of the death of the owner, the executor or person entitled to electronic bonds just needs to contact TreasuryDirect referencing the owner's TreasuryDirect account number to begin the process of transferring ownership of the bonds. With paper bonds you get less help in this situation.

See Book Note 6-1 for the email address of TreasuryDirect.

★ Paper Savings Bonds require that a bank officer certify the identity of bond holders. With electronic bonds, knowledge of a TreasuryDirect account number and password is considered proof of identity. Consequently, anyone with the password is effectively a "co-owner", although their name isn't on the registration. ***This is the case even when the password is obtained fraudulently! You must handle your account number and password with great care.***

How to open a new TreasuryDirect account

TreasuryDirect is an online service offered by the U.S. Treasury. You can use it to buy and hold either Savings Bonds or marketable Treasury securities (T-Bills, T-Notes, T-Bonds, TIPS).

There is also an older system, called **Legacy Treasury Direct**, that only handles marketable securities, not Savings Bonds. It's being phased out. This chapter is about the newer, better TreasuryDirect.

In order to open an account, you need the following six pieces of information. Note that there are no citizenship requirements:
- ★ Social Security Number
- ★ Address in the United States
- ★ Driver's license – or, if don't drive, a state ID
- ★ Account (checking or savings) at a bank in the United States – you'll need to know the routing numbers to your account
- ★ Email address
- ★ Web browser that supports 128-bit encryption

The process for opening a TreasuryDirect account is to enter your personal information, such as name and address, as well as the information listed above. You will also select a password, a password reminder, and additional authentication information. You will also have an opportunity to read the TreasuryDirect terms and conditions and privacy and legal notices.

After you submit this information, the Treasury will email the account number of your new account to you within 24 hours. If you don't receive it, try again. You will need the account number and the password you selected to log in to your new account.

The URL is **www.TreasuryDirect.gov**

There's more on bank routing numbers and on web browsers coming up.

Or you can go to our web site, click on Book Notes, and see:

Note 6-2: Terms and conditions
Note 6-3: Privacy and legal notices
Note 6-4: Open an account

Will your browser work with TreasuryDirect?

Most current browsers support the level of encryption needed to use TreasuryDirect.

In fact, if your browser doesn't support this level of encryption, it may be difficult for you to upgrade, because the latest browsers may require a newer operating system than you have on your computer.

To determine what version of browser you have:

★ **Windows**: Select the bottom item in the list that drops down from your browser's *Help* menu

★ **Macintosh**: If you have a newer Mac with OS X, your browser will work. If you have an older Mac with System 10 or earlier: With your browser open and active, select the first item in the list that drops down from your *Apple* menu (look in the top-left corner of your screen)

In either case, the window that opens will give you the browser's version number. It may also tell you the level of **encryption cipher strength** supported – you need 128-bit or higher. The following versions support this level of encryption:

★ **Internet Explorer** – version 5.01 or newer

★ **Netscape** – version 6.2 or newer

★ **Mozilla Firefox** – version 1.0 or newer

TreasuryDirect uses a security certificate from a company called Entrust, which keeps a detailed list of supported browsers and their security vulnerabilities. See Book Note 6-8.

For the latest version of Internet Explorer, go to our web site, click on Book Notes, and see note 6-5.

For the latest versions of the Mozilla Firefox browser, see note 6-6.

For the latest version of the Opera browser, see note 6-7.

For Entrust's list of supported browsers, see note 6-8.

Bank Routing Numbers

You can always call your bank and ask for the routing numbers to your account, but if you have a check or deposit slip, just look at the funny numbers at the bottom.

The first group of numbers will begin and end with a character that looks like a vertical line followed by two dots, one on top of the other. The numbers in between these characters are your bank routing number.

The second group begins and ends with a character that looks like two vertical lines followed by a single dot. The numbers between these characters are your bank account number.

Checks may have a third group of characters, which give the check number. (And cancelled checks will have a fourth group of numbers, which is the amount of the check). You can ignore these.

Using your TreasuryDirect account

Once you have opened an account, you can log into it from anywhere and:

* buy new bonds
* schedule future one-time or periodic purchases
* redeem the electronic bonds you own
* create registrations for others and buy gift bonds for them
* transfer your own bonds to accounts belonging to others
* change the beneficiary on your bonds
* set up accounts for specific purposes, such as an education or wedding fund for your kids, that are linked to your main account
* check up on the current interest rate and current value of your bonds.

WARNING: if you receive an email that appears to be from the Treasury asking you to log into TreasuryDirect or asking for your account number and password, **stop!** Instead, log into TreasuryDirect by typing in the URL, *www.treasurydirect.gov.* Use the *Contact Us* link to report the email, which is fraudulent. The Treasury will never send you an email like this.

To access your account, go to *www.treasurydirect.gov.*

If you've forgotten your account number or password, there are links on the login page to help you recover it.

When you log into TreasuryDirect, you're initially asked to enter the first character of your account number. On the next screen, you enter your account number and password. Include that first character again as part of your account number on the second screen or you won't be able to log in.

Or go to our web site, click on Book Notes, and see note 6-9.

TreasuryDirect deposit option

Your employer, pension fund, or anyone else who sends you money regularly can deposit a part of the money into TreasuryDirect.

Once inside your TreasuryDirect account, the deposits appear in what the Treasury calls a *Zero-Percent Certificate of Indebtedness*. This is basically a holding area for your money inside TreasuryDirect.

From within TreasuryDirect, you can put additional money into your certificate by creating an electronic withdrawal from your bank account or by redeeming Savings Bonds you already have.

You can take money out of your certificate either by creating an electronic deposit into your bank account or investing in Savings Bonds or other Treasury securities.

To transfer paycheck deductions into your TreasuryDirect account, give your payroll office or financial institution the following information:

★ Bank name: TREASURYDIRECT (all caps, no spaces)
★ TreasuryDirect's Routing Number: 051736158
★ Your ten-digit TreasuryDirect account number
★ Account type: savings
★ The amount to be deducted
★ The frequency for the deduction

As you can tell from the name, a *Zero-Percent Certificate of Indebtedness* doesn't earn interest, so make sure you set up transactions in TreasuryDirect to move the money into Savings Bonds or other Treasury securities.

How to convert paper bonds to electronic bonds

If you have both a TreasuryDirect account and paper bonds, you can put your paper bonds into your TreasuryDirect account, which will convert them to electronic bonds.

First, log onto your TreasuryDirect account. Click on the *Manage Direct* button, which is in the middle of the row of blue buttons at the top of the page. On the page that appears, there should be a set of options called *Manage My Conversions*.

The conversion feature is being introduced gradually. If you don't have it yet, click the *Contact Us* link at the top-right of the page and ask the Treasury to add the feature to your account.

The next step is to sort your paper Savings Bonds into groups based on how they're registered. Bonds that have different co-owners or beneficiaries should go into separate groups.

When you've completed that step, log back on to your TreasuryDirect account, go back to *Manage Direct,* and click on *Access My Conversion Linked Account.*

On that page, click on *Create my registration list* and enter the registration information for each of the groups you've created.

After you've created your list of registrations, enter each of your bonds. You'll select the registration on the bond from the list you've created and enter the series, denomination, and serial number. You will also be able to enter comments, such as a note about a name change or misspelling.

When you've finished entering your bonds, click the button labeled *Create a Manifest*. This will display a list of all the bonds you've entered. You'll need to print this, sign it, and mail it with the bonds to the address shown on the manifest. You can put up to 50 bonds on one manifest, and you can have as many manifests as you need.

The bonds will be listed in your TreasuryDirect account, where you'll be able to see their current value and interest rate. You'll also be able to check on the status of your conversions to see if processing is proceeding normally or if a problem has occurred.

Part II – Managing your investment

Savings Bond A, B, Cs

How much are my Savings Bonds worth?

Keeping track of your Savings Bond inventory

Savings Bonds and estate planning

Inheriting Savings Bonds

Changing the registration

Lost and stolen Savings Bonds

Chapter 7

Savings Bond A, B, Cs

Before I and EE came A, B, C, D....

Understanding rate periods

Understanding maturity periods

Series E and EE Savings Bonds issued before May 2005

The guaranteed rate feature of older Savings Bonds

Series H and HH feature current income

Before I and EE came A, B, C, D....

Like New York City subway lines, Savings Bonds use letters to identify their series. Bonds in Series A, B, C, D, F, G, J, and K are not only no longer sold - they no longer earn interest and should be cashed in.

The one Savings Bond Series that doesn't have a letter - bonds in this series are sometimes called *Savings Notes* and sometimes *Freedom Shares* - has also stopped earning interest and should be cashed in.

You may also hear the terms *Patriot Bond* and *Gulf Coast Recovery Bond*, however, these aren't official Savings Bond series.

Since December 11, 2001, all paper Series EE bonds purchased at financial institutions - but not those purchased through Payroll Savings Plans - have been called Patriot Bonds. These bonds are identical to other Series EE bonds except for the words *Patriot Bond* printed on the top half of the bond between the social security number and issue date.

The Patriot Bond is just a standard Series EE bond with the Patriot Bond wording on the front.

Likewise a *Gulf Coast Recovery Bond* is a Series I bond issued from March 29 through the end of December, 2006.

Series I and Series EE are the only two series of Savings Bonds that the Treasury now offers. We described the current features of the Series I and EE bonds in Chapter 1 and Chapter 3.

Older issues of Series EE bonds have different rules and features than those issued now. In addition, there are three series of Savings Bonds - Series E, H, and HH - that are no longer issued but in some cases are still earning interest. Before we dive into learning about these types of Savings Bonds, however, we need to make sure your understand *rate periods* and *maturity periods*.

Understanding rate periods

Savings Bonds pay a wide variety of interest rates, depending on their series and issue date. To understand how they work, you have to understand the concept of **rate periods**.

Every Savings Bond has a series of six-month rate periods that begin with the month in which the bond is issued. Today's Savings Bonds pay interest for 30 years, so they have 60 rate periods.

What's confusing is that the Treasury announces new interest rates for Savings Bonds in May and November, but the announced rates don't apply to a specific Saving Bond until its next rate period begins, which is zero (for bonds purchased in May or November) to five (for bonds purchased in April or October) months later.

Flip the page and take a quick look at Figure 7-1. It's a time line, with the months, shown in the third column, running down the page.

A bond issued in January (column four) has a January-June rate period and a July-December rate period. A bond issued in May (column eight) has May-October and November-April rate periods.

If a bond's rate changes, the change always occurs between one rate period and the next one, never during a rate period.

The Treasury announces new Savings Bond rates on the first business days of May and November. The horizontal lines in Figure 7-1 represent these announcement dates.

It's important that you understand how the two announcements match up with each of your bonds' two annual rate periods.

Most people assume that the rates announced in May and November apply to all Savings Bonds as of Nov 1 and May 1. Whoops – it doesn't work that way at all.

The announced rates do apply to all *new* Savings Bond investments as of May 1 and November 1. However, for older bonds, the announced rates aren't used until a bond's next rate period begins.

In Figure 7-1, notice that for a bond issued in February or August (column five), the November rate announcement is applied beginning the following February. The May rate announcement is applied beginning the following August.

Note that for a Savings Bond purchased in April or October (column 7), the rate announced in November applies to a rate period that begins five months after – and ends eleven months after – the rate announcement.

Moreover, the I bond announcement is based on the average inflation rate for the six-month period that ends *the month before* the announcement.

These features create a rate lag that confuses most of the Savings Bond investors I talk to.

One more thing – the announced rates are expressed as an annual rate, but the rate periods only last half a year.

You'll earn one-half of the announced rate for your bond's first six-month rate period, then you'll earn one-half of the next announced rate for your bond's second six-month rate period.

Now study Figure 7-1. Figure out when the rate periods begin for some of your own bonds. How far behind the rate announcement do their rates lag?

When the rate-period light comes on for you, you're ready to move on and learn about maturity periods.

Rate periods are a little complicated, but essential for a Savings Bond investor to understand.

Figure 7-1

Savings Bond rate-setting and interest-earning rate periods

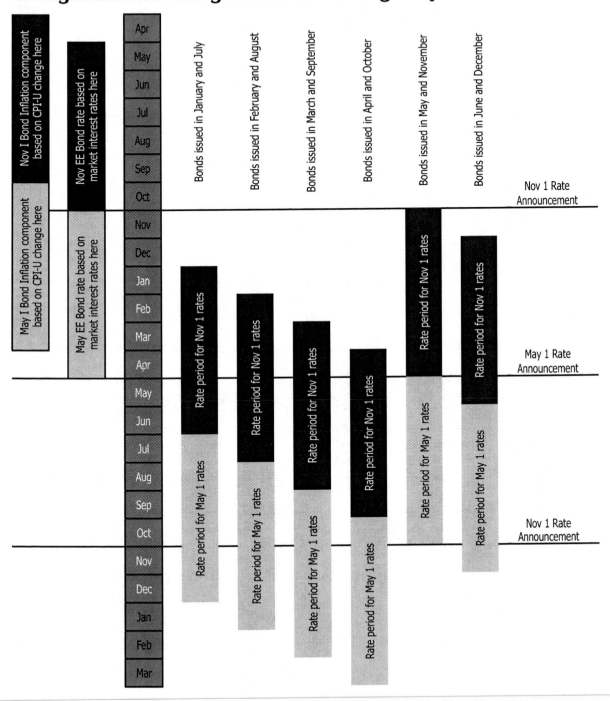

Understanding maturity periods

Series I bonds don't have maturity periods. All other series do.

For H and HH bonds, each maturity period lasts ten years. When an H or HH bond moves from one maturity period to another, the Treasury has an opportunity to change its interest rate.

For E and EE bonds, the length of the first maturity period is connected to the bond's *original maturity guarantee*. The Treasury guarantees these bonds will reach face value in their first maturity period.

Because the Treasury lengthened the original maturity period by six years in March 1993, the next time one of these boosts to face value could occur is in March 2011.

Table 7-1 shows the original maturity guarantees of all EE bonds ever issued. The table shows issue dates, the length of the maturity period, the effective interest rate the original maturity guarantee creates, and whether the guarantee is complete or not.

Table 7-1

Series EE Original Maturity Guarantees

Issue Date	Original Term	Interest Rate	Complete?
Jan 80 — Oct 80	11 years	6.40%	yes
Nov 80 — Apr 81	9 years	7.85%	yes
May 81 — Oct 82	8 years	8.85%	yes
Nov 82 — Oct 86	10 years	7.05%	yes
Nov 86 — Feb 93	12 years	5.86%	yes
Mar 93 — Apr 95	18 years	3.89%	no
May 95 — May 03	17 years	4.12%	no
Jun 03 — present	20 years	3.50%	no

The length of an EE bond's original maturity period is set when the bond is issued. As the table shows, currently new EE bonds have an original maturity guarantee of 20 years.

Since Series EE Savings Bonds pay interest for 30 years, these bonds will have a second and final maturity period of ten years. As with H and HH bonds, the Treasury has the right to change an EE bond's interest rate when it passes from one maturity period to another.

As you can see, older EE bonds had original maturity periods in a number of different lengths. In this case, the original maturity period was followed by one or two ten-year maturity periods and a final maturity period.

For example, if a bond pays interest for 30 years and the original maturity period was nine years, the second was ten years, the third ten years, and the final one year. If the original maturity period was twelve years, the second was ten years, and the final was eight years.

Series E and EE Savings Bonds issued before May 2005

Unlike the fixed rates of the current Series EE, older Series EE and Series E Savings Bonds pay interest rates that adjust every six months based on the prevailing level of interest rates in the bond market.

However, the exact method of determining this adjustable rate depends on when a bond was issued.

May 1997 through April 2005 issue dates

The Series EE Savings Bonds issued during this eight-year period have the following differences from bonds issued now:

★ The interest rate paid by these bonds changes every six months.

★ The interest rate for each six-month rate period is 90% of the average yield for five-year Treasury securities during the previous six months.

★ These bonds have an active *original maturity guarantee.*
  ★ Bonds issued from June 2003 to April 2005 are guaranteed to double in value in 20 years, which creates an annual yield of 3.5% for bonds held that long.
  ★ Bonds issued from May 1997 to May 2003 are guaranteed to double in value in 17 years, which creates an annual yield of 4.12%.

May 1995 through April 1997 issue dates

The Series EE Savings Bonds issued during this two-year period have the following differences from bonds issued previously:

★ The interest rate for each six-month rate period is 85% (rather than 90%) of the average yield for five-year Treasury securities.

★ Interest accrues (is added to the bond's value for redemption calculations) twice a year rather than monthly. This creates the hidden interest rate penalty discussed in Chapter 16. The accrual dates are the first business day of the bond's issue month and six months later. For example, a bond issued in January jumps in value on January 1 and July 1.

★ The original maturity guarantee on these bonds is 17 years or 4.12%.

Issue dates prior to May 1995

Series E and Series EE Savings Bonds issued before May 1995 have the following differences from bonds issued more recently:

★ Interest rates are calculated two different ways. At redemption, the method that provides the highest return is used to calculate the value of the bond.

   ★ The first method is based on *guaranteed rates* during the life of the bond.

   ★ The second method is based on the average of the market-based rates (85% of the average yield for 5-year Treasury securities) published during the life of the bond.

★ Consequently, the interest earned during any particular month depends on which of the two methods will give the bond the highest value.

   ★ If the first method is best, the bond will earn whatever rate is required to make its value reach the guaranteed rates in effect during its life.

   ★ If the second method is best, the bond will earn whatever rate is required to make its value reach the average of the market-based rates published during its life.

★ Interest accrues (is added to the bond's value for redemption calculations) twice a year, at the beginning of the month of issue and six months later.

All Savings Bonds issued before May 1997 accrue interest semiannually.

This creates a potential redemption penalty of up to six-months interest that most people don't know about. We discuss how to avoid this penalty in Chapter 16.

★ The original maturity guarantee on these bonds is complete – the bonds have already reached face value – except for bonds issued in April 1995 and before that are less than 18 years old. These bonds double in value in 18 years, which creates a yield guarantee of 3.89%.

★ Stops earning interest:
  ★ Series E issued before Dec 1965 – 40 years
  ★ Series EE and Series E issued Dec 1965 and since – 30 years

★ Purchase price:
  ★ Series E – sold at 75% of face value (you paid $75 for a $100 bond)
  ★ Series EE – sold at 50% of face value (you paid $50 for a $100 bond)

★ Issue Dates:
  ★ Series E – first issued in May 1941, last issued in June 1980
  ★ Series EE – first issued in January 1980 – note the six-month overlap with Series E issue dates in the first half of 1980

★ Denominations:
  ★ Series E – in addition to the face-value denominations offered by Series EE and I bonds ($50, $75, $100, $200, $500, $1,000, $5,000, $10,000), Series E bonds were available in $10 and $25 denominations.

The guaranteed rate feature of older bonds

As we've seen, Series E and EE bonds issued prior to May 1995 have a feature called guaranteed rates. Most of these bonds are actually earning their guaranteed rate, so let's look at this feature in a bit more detail.

The most important thing to understand is that the guarantee applies to the bond's current maturity period, not to each of the six-month rate periods within the maturity period.

Consequently, a bond that earns more than its guaranteed rate early in a maturity period can earn less than its guaranteed rate later in the maturity period and still meet the guarantee over the maturity period as a whole.

This is why some Savings Bonds earn less than their guaranteed rate in specific six-month rate periods.

As discussed earlier in this chapter, when older bonds move from one maturity period to the next, the Treasury can adjust their guaranteed rate.

The Treasury's guaranteed rate for an E or EE bond moving into a new maturity period has been 4% since March 1993. That's long enough ago that all Series E and EE bonds that have guaranteed rates currently have a guaranteed rate of 4%.

Series H and HH feature current income

Series HH Savings Bonds, as well as the older Series H bonds, are no longer issued. They are substantially different from Series I and EE bonds in that their interest is sent to you – typically by direct deposit into your bank account – rather than added to the value of the bond, as with all other Savings Bonds.

The payment is made in the issue month of the bond and six months later. If you have moved, changed banks, or inherited Series H or HH bonds, it's possible that you're not receiving interest payments that are owed to you. We'll discuss how to solve this problem in a moment.

When they were available, the only way to obtain H / HH bonds was in exchange for E / EE bonds or matured H /HH bonds.

Income tax on the interest earned by the E / EE bonds that were exchanged for the H / HH bonds is deferred until the H / HH bonds are redeemed or until they reach final maturity and stop earning interest.

On the face of an HH bond you'll see an entry called *deferred interest*. This is the amount of interest that you will have to pay income tax on when the bond is redeemed or stops earning interest.

On the other hand, unlike other Savings Bonds, you pay income tax on the interest these bonds pay to you in cash in the year in which you receive it.

The redemption value of these bonds is always their face value. Although there was a minimum holding period for HH bonds, it's long past and all H and HH bonds are redeemable.

At redemption, the 1099-INT tax form reporting the interest to you and the IRS is issued using the Social Security Number of the primary owner – the person whose name appears first in the registration (with other paper bonds, the SSN of the person cashing the bond is used).

If you have a large investment in Series E / EE or H / HH bonds that will stop paying interest in the next few years, you are sitting on a deferred-tax time bomb. See Chapter 17.

All H / HH bonds have a hidden interest-rate penalty you can easily avoid if you understand when to redeem your bonds. See Chapter 16.

H and HH bonds have ten-year maturity periods. The rate paid by a new bond was set for the first ten years when it was issued and is reset at the end of each ten-year period to the then-current rate, which is currently a meager 1.5%.

Series H / HH bonds were issued at full face value (you paid $500 for a $500 bond) and came in four denominations: $500, $1,000, $5,000, and $10,000.

Series H bonds were first issued in June 1952 and earn interest for 30 years. They were replaced by Series HH Savings Bonds in January 1980. Series HH bonds earn interest for 20 years. They were last issued in August 2004.

Inheriting Series H and HH Savings Bonds

Chapter 11 discusses the forms to use to have Savings Bonds reregistered when you inherit them or are Executor of the estate of a Savings Bond owner. The same forms are used for Series H and HH Savings Bonds.

However, timely reregistration is more important if the deceased person owned Series H or HH bonds. That's because the semiannual interest payments are being deposited in his or her bank account, which you will be closing.

In order to get the payments going to the correct account, follow the reregistration instructions in Chapter 11.

Missing interest payments

If you aren't receiving interest payments on an H or HH Savings Bond, notify the following office in writing, including your HH bond registration information, face values, and serial numbers and they will work with you to correct the situation:

H / HH Assistance Branch
Bureau of the Public Debt
PO Box 2186
Parkersburg WV 26106-2186

Direct deposit of interest payments

If you are receiving your Series H / HH interest payments by check, you can use the Treasury's **Public Debt Form 5396** – *Direct Deposit Sign-Up Form* – to sign up for direct deposit.

Changing your direct-deposit bank account

If you want to change the bank account your HH interest payments are going into, use the same *Deposit Sign Up Form*. The form doesn't say on it anywhere that it can be used to change the bank account your interest payments are going to, but the Treasury says it's the right form for this.

Check the *Interest Payments* box at the top of the form. The instructions on the form are ambiguous about whether you need to include the bonds with your request – you don't. Unlike most Savings Bond forms, you don't even have to have your signature certified by a bank.

Treasury web site for Series HH Savings Bonds

The Treasury has an internet site for Series H / HH Savings Bond owners. You can access the site using the Social Security Number and the Serial Number on one of your H / HH bonds. The site allows you to:
- ★ view your accounts
- ★ change your address
- ★ request tax information

We have a link to this site at Book Note 7-2 on our web site. The H / HH site is available:
- ★ Monday-Friday, 8 am to 8 pm Eastern time
- ★ Saturday, 7 am to 2:30 pm Eastern time
- ★ (excluding federal holidays)

For the Direct Deposit sign up form, see the Appendix or go to our web site, click on Book Notes, and see note 7-1.

To link to the Treasury's web site for Series H / HH bonds, go to our web site, click on Book Notes, and see note 7-2.

Chapter 8

How much are my Savings Bonds worth?

Looking up a bond's rate and value using our tables

Savings Bond Advisor rate and value calculator

Rates and values in TreasuryDirect

Savings Bond Calculator

Savings Bond Wizard

Looking up a bond's rate and value using our tables

Earlier editions of this book included tables in the back that allowed readers to look up the current rate or redemption value of any Savings Bond.

Because this meant we had to issue a new edition every six months and because book stores couldn't keep up with new editions flying out the door that rapidly, we've removed the tables from the book and made them available online.

Book Note 8-1 will allow you download an Adobe Acrobat (.pdf) file with the current version of these tables. The file begins with instructions about how to read the tables.

Book Note 8-1 will take you to an online version of the Savings Bond rate and value tables that were included in the back of earlier editions of this book.

Savings Bond Advisor rate and value calculator

In addition to the tables on our web site, you have several other online choices for determining the current rate and redemption values of your Savings Bonds.

The simplest of these is the Savings Bond rate and value calculator on our web site. You'll find a small version of the calculator, shown in Figure 8-1, at the upper right on almost every page of the site.

To use the calculator, just enter the face value, series, and issue month and year of your Savings Bond and click the *Calculate Value* button.

This will move you to a different page on the web site, shown in Figure 8-2, that has a similar entry pad with more instructions and the results for your request.

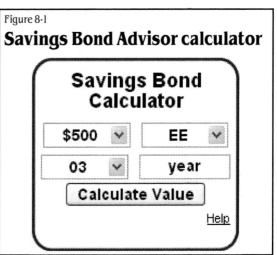

Figure 8-1

Savings Bond Advisor calculator

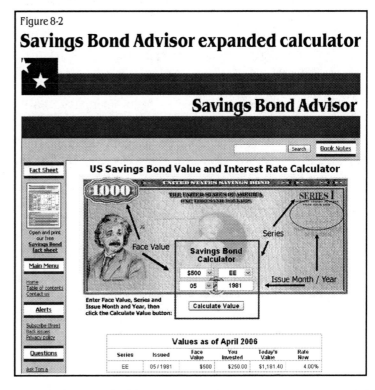

Figure 8-2

Savings Bond Advisor expanded calculator

The Savings Bond Guru

The Savings Bond Guru is commercial online software that provides important features the Treasury's Savings Bond programs lack.

Like the Treasury's Savings Bond Wizard, but unlike other online calculators, the Savings Bond Guru remembers the bond data you enter.

But the Savings Bond Wizard saves your bond data in a file on your own computer. The Savings Bond Guru saves it on its own systems. This means that the Guru both backs up your data offsite and is able to do new calculations at a later time.

The Savings Bond Guru's major feature is that it emails you a monthly statement about your Savings Bond portfolio. The Treasury never sends you anything equivalent to what banks, mutual funds, and brokers send out on a monthly basis. The Savings Bond Guru is a very inexpensive way to get this service.

You don't have to worry about losing your data when you change computers. You don't have to worry about data updates every six months. It's all automatic. All you have to do is remember - and protect - your password.

It's a lot easier to sign up for the Savings Bond Guru than to download and install the Treasury's Wizard. You have to fill out a little form with your email address, password, name, and zip code, but it takes just a few seconds to begin entering your Savings Bonds and seeing what they're worth.

For more information and a link to the Guru, go to our web site, use our Savings Bond rate and value calculator, and look in the area below the results.

Rates and values in TreasuryDirect

TreasuryDirect provides a summary of your Savings Bond holdings and their current rates and values. Once you've logged in to TreasuryDirect, click on the *Current Holdings* button and you'll see a page that looks like Figure 8-3.

The value shown in the **Amount** column is how much you've invested and the value in the **Current Value** column is what your investment is worth now.

If you click on one of the radio buttons shown in the top figure and then on *Submit*, you'll see a **Current Holdings >> Summary** page, as shown in Figure 8-4.

This page shows you not only how much you've invested (**Amount**) and the **Current Value** of your investment, it also shows you the issue dates and current interest rate for each of your holdings. However, it doesn't show the fixed base-rate for I bonds.

Don't forget you can now convert your paper bonds to electronic and track all your Savings Bonds in TreasuryDirect. See Chapter 6 for complete information.

Figure 8-3

TreasuryDirect – current holdings

Figure 8-4

TreasuryDirect – holdings summary

Savings Bond Calculator

The Treasury provides two additional ways to find out the value of your paper Savings Bonds – the *Savings Bond Calculator* and the *Savings Bond Wizard*.

The *Savings Bond Calculator* is a web-based program that works on any computer system that has a web browser. The *Savings Bond Wizard*, on the other hand, requires a Windows computer and that you have the ability and willingness to install new software on it. If you're okay with that, the *Wizard* offers more features and is the better choice.

Book Note 8-3 links to the *Savings Bond Calculator*. Figure 8-5 shows you what it looks like after you've entered two bonds.

You enter the information on your bonds at the top. When you click the *Calculate* button, it adds three lines of information about that bond in the table at the bottom. In between is a section that shows your total investment, its redemption value, and the interest it has earned – both since you invested and for the current year.

The *How to Save Your Inventory* button takes you to a page of instructions about how to save your inventory after you have entered it so that you don't have to enter it again the next time you want to see the value of your bonds.

Unfortunately, the method for saving data is very different from your other software, as is the method for reloading it next time you want to take a look at your portfolio.

Or if you are a Linux user, **GBonds** is a free downloadable program you can use. For more info, go to our web site, click on Book Notes, and see Note 8-2.

To run the Treasury's Savings Bond Calculator, go to our web site, click on Book Notes, and see note 8-3.

Figure 8-5

Savings Bond Calculator with two entries

Calculate the Value of Your Paper Savings Bond(s)

SAVINGS BOND CALCULATOR

Value as of:
11/2006   **UPDATE**   Help

Series: Denomination: Bond Serial Number: Issue Date:
I Bonds   1,000

CALCULATE   **HOW TO SAVE YOUR INVENTORY**

Calculator Results for Redemption Date 11/2006

VIEW/PRINT/SAVE LIST

Total Price: Total Value: Total Interest: YTD Interest:
$2,000.00 $3,246.00 $1,246.00 $221.20

Bonds: 1-2 of 2

Serial #	13 characters	Issue Date	10/1998	Issue Price	$1,000.00	Value	$1,620.00
Series	I	Next Accrual	12/2006	Interest	$620.00	Note	
Denom	$1,000	Final Maturity	10/2028	Interest Rate	4.42%	REMOVE	

Serial #	13 characters	Issue Date	09/1998	Issue Price	$1,000.00	Value	$1,626.00
Series	I	Next Accrual	12/2006	Interest	$626.00	Note	
Denom	$1,000	Final Maturity	09/2028	Interest Rate	4.42%	REMOVE	

Savings Bond Wizard

After you download, install, and run the Treasury's *Savings Bond Wizard* and make some entries, it will look something like the display in Figure 8-6.

Compared to the *Savings Bond Calculator*, the *Wizard* makes it easy to save and reload one or several portfolios, it allows you to enter multiple bonds at once (see **Easy Inventory Builder** in the **Tools** menu), and it provides a number of reports that allow you to look at your portfolio in different ways. You can edit your entries and you can mark bonds as redeemed without deleting them.

Downloading and Installing the Savings Bond Wizard

The current version of the Treasury's *Savings Bond Wizard* is 4.13. If you've downloaded the *Wizard* before, you can see if you have the current version by selecting **About the Wizard...** from the **Help** menu.

The *Savings Bond Wizard* runs on any Windows-based computer except very old models that use a system prior to Windows 95. The *Wizard* requires less than 3 megabytes of disk space.

Figure 8-6

Savings Bond Wizard with two entries

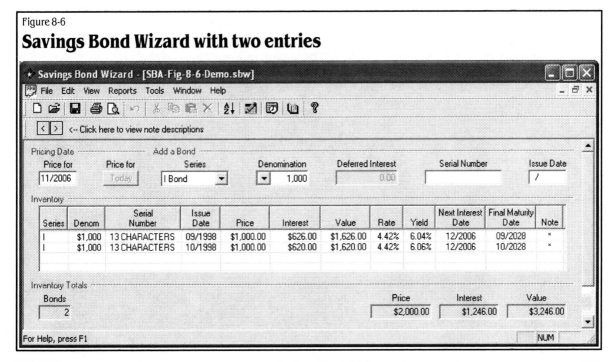

To download it, go to our web site, click on Book Notes, and select Note 8-4. The download link on our web site will link you to the web site of the Bureau of Public Debt at the U.S. Treasury. You will download the file from their site, not ours.

When you follow the link, you will see a standard *Save Dialog Window* – create a new folder or select an existing one to save the file – **sbwsetup.exe** – on your own computer.

After you have downloaded the file, select the **Run...** command from your **Start** menu. Click on the *Browse* button, find the file you just downloaded, select it, then click the *OK* button. If you have administrative rights to install software on your computer, you'll be seconds away from using the *Wizard*.

The installation process will put a link to the *Savings Bond Wizard* in your **Start** menu. When the installation process is complete, find the *Wizard* in your **Start** menu and crank it up.

Updating your inventory

A major disadvantage of the *Savings Bond Wizard* is that it needs to download updated information on interest rates and values every six months. As you might guess, new data is available in early May and November.

While your computer is connected to the Internet, select **Redemption Values** from the **Tools** menu. In the window that appears, click the *Automatic Update* button. The *Wizard* will grab the latest files from the Treasury's web site for you.

To download the Treasury's Savings Bond Wizard, go to our web site, click on Book Notes, and see note 8-4.

Chapter 9

Keeping track of your Savings Bond inventory

Controlling the biggest risk of Savings Bonds

The best way to keep a Savings Bond inventory

Other ways to keep a Savings Bond inventory

Controlling the biggest risk of Savings Bonds

As discussed elsewhere in this book, Savings Bonds are a very safe investment. However, they carry one risk few other investments share – ***the risk that you'll forget you own them***.

As impossible as this sounds, over 5% of all Savings Bonds outstanding are no longer earning interest and haven't been redeemed. Here's why.

You can't depend on the Treasury to notify you when your Savings Bonds stop earning interest. The Treasury does have a very small team that tries to contact owners of Savings Bonds that have stopped earning interest, but unless you have an unusual name that they can trace you are unlikely to hear from them.

When you own stocks, mutual funds, or other investments, you receive at least an annual report reminding you – and your heirs after you're gone – of those assets. The Treasury doesn't provide anything like this for Savings Bonds.

In this chapter we'll look at some ways you can control this risk by keeping an inventory of the Savings Bonds you've purchased and redeemed.

Find a safe place to keep your inventory

No matter which of these methods you use, it's important to keep your inventory and your actual Savings Bonds in different locations. Some of the risk of losing your Savings Bonds comes from disasters like fire and storms. If everything is in one location you can lose both at the same time.

For example, besides home, work, and a bank safe deposit box, you could ask a relative or lawyer to keep a copy of your bond inventory for you. If you have registered the Savings Bonds with a co-owner or beneficiary who doesn't live with you, it would be good to give him or her a copy of the inventory.

In any case, make sure that your heirs know that you own Savings Bonds and that they'll be able to find an up-to-date inventory of your holdings with your other financial paperwork.

The best way to keep a Savings Bond inventory

The ideal Savings Bond inventory would keep track of all your Savings Bonds in a location that's safe and private but not the same place that your Savings Bonds are stored.

In addition, the ideal inventory method would automatically update the value and interest rates of your Savings Bonds without making you track down update files or re-enter your data.

An ideal system would include additional information on each of your bonds, such as the best time to redeem them, which of your Savings Bonds are about to change in value, and which have stopped earning interest.

The ideal system should also send you automatic updates – something like the monthly statements you get from your other investment accounts.

If you're interested in the ideal system, go to our web site, use our Savings Bond Calculator, and look in the area below the results for information on *The Savings Bond Guru*, a service that provides all these features.

Other ways to keep a Savings Bond inventory

Here are four other ways to keep an inventory of your Savings Bonds.

The photocopy method

This one's really simple if you only have paper bonds – just photocopy each of your bonds on a separate piece of paper and put all the photocopies in a folder. If you're the paperless type, you can scan the bonds and keep the images in a computer file.

The big advantage of this method is that you will capture all the data about each bond - registration, face value, issue date, and serial number. There's no chance of typographical or transcription errors.

It's easy to add new bonds to your inventory by slipping a new photocopy into your folder.

When you redeem bonds, rather than removing the photocopy of that bond, keep it. Just make a note in writing on that sheet that you've redeemed the bond. This will keep you from wondering someday whether you cashed it or not.

You can use the blank space on each sheet to write in things such as current values, interest rates, when the bond will stop earning interest, best days for redemption, and the Alert Recommendation – all of which you can get from the tables in Book Note 8-1 on our web site.

The disadvantage of this method is that it doesn't summarize the total value of the inventory for you. But you can combine it with others methods, such as,...

The spreadsheet method

You can use just a pencil and blank sheet of paper to write down all the important information on your Savings Bonds, but if you have Microsoft Excel, we've created a simple spreadsheet you can download. Go to our web site and select Book Note 9-1.

If you want to stick with paper, lay out 15 columns on the sheet. Here are the titles to use for the 15 columns (the spreadsheet template has an extra column that calculates the current value for you after you enter the *Value per $* from our tables at Book Note 8-1):

- ★ First Owner
- ★ OR or POD
- ★ Second Owner or Beneficiary
- ★ Social Security Number
- ★ Serial Number
- ★ Type (paper or TreasuryDirect)
- ★ Series
- ★ Issue Date
- ★ Face Value
- ★ Deferred Interest (H and HH only)
- ★ Current interest rate (from online tables)
- ★ Current Value (face values times *Value per $* from online tables)
- ★ To avoid rate penalty, redeem (from online tables)
- ★ Lifetime APY (from online tables)
- ★ Alert Recommendation (from online tables)
- ★ Stops paying interest (from online tables)

The advantage of this method is that you will develop a familiarity with your bonds. The disadvantage, of course, is that it's a lot of work.

The TreasuryDirect method

If you own only electronic bonds, you can just print out the TreasuryDirect pages that show your holdings and their current values and interest rates.

TreasuryDirect is fully covered in Chapter 6.

Owners of paper bonds can also use this method by converting their bonds to electronic bonds, as described in Chapter 6.

A Savings Bond Wizard inventory

If you're using the *Savings Bond Wizard*, you'll want to check out its **Reports** menu. This menu lists a wide variety of reports you can run and print out. Reports are a feature that the Treasury's *Savings Bond Wizard* provides but the online *Savings Bond Calculator* doesn't.

Reports that would come up empty are dim in the menu – for example, if you haven't marked any bonds as cashed in, the *Bonds Cashed In* report will be dim and you won't be able to select it.

One of the most useful reports provided by the *Savings Bond Wizard* is the *Active Inventory* report, shown in Figure 9-1. This report lists all of your unredeemed bonds, including their serial numbers, if you have entered them. One disadvantage of this report, which you can overcome with handwritten notes or a photocopy inventory, is that it doesn't include any of the registration information on your bonds.

You can read all about the Savings Bond Wizard in Chapter 8.

Figure 9-1

Savings Bond Wizard – Active Inventory Report

Inventory Report
Active Inventory

Print Date: 09/03/2004

Bonds:

File Pricing Date: 11/2004

No.	Series	Denom	Serial Number	Issue Date	Price	Interest [Deferred]	Value	Rate	Yield	Next Interest Date	Final Maturity Date	Note
1	E	$1,000	X0000000E	09/1978	$750.00	$2,902.00	$3,652.00	4.00%	6.18%	03/2005	09/2008	
2	EE	1,000	X0000000EE	09/1988	500.00	691.20	1,191.20	4.00%	5.50%	03/2005	09/2018	
3	I	1,000		09/1998	1,000.00	419.60	1,419.60	5.82%	5.76%	12/2004	09/2028	*
4	HH	1,000	UP TO 13 CHRS	09/1998	1,000.00	[800.00]	1,000.00	4.00%		03/2005	09/2018	
5	I	50		10/2000	50.00	13.14	63.14	6.02%	5.80%	12/2004	10/2030	P5*

Inventory Totals:

Bonds		Deferred Interest		Price	Interest	Value
5		$800.00		$3,300.00	$4,025.94	$7,325.94

Chapter 10

Savings Bonds and estate planning

What is estate planning?

Minimizing taxes when passing on Savings Bonds

Co-owner / beneficiary pros and cons

Other estate planning issues

What is estate planning?

Your *estate* can be thought of as a temporary entity that owns your property during the period between your death and when distribution of your property to your heirs is complete.

Estate planning involves figuring out ahead of time what you want to happen to your property when you die and then executing the proper legal documents to ensure things happen that way.

Your death will be a traumatic experience for your family. By planning ahead you can minimize family disputes and confusion, speed distribution of your assets, and lower the legal fees and taxes your family will have to pay.

What is probate?

When someone dies owning property or financial assets, a Probate Court has the responsibility to determine who the decedent's heirs are and to see that the decedent's property and assets are legally distributed to the heirs.

If you have a Will, the court will examine it and hear arguments about its validity. If you don't leave a Will, the court will follow the laws in your state to determine the disposition of your property.

The court's determination, including specific information about the character and value of your estate, becomes part of the public record.

The probate process typically takes six to twelve months but can take longer if the estate is complex or if there are disagreements about the Will.

The court will appoint an executor to manage the estate and the probate process. The executor will typically hire a lawyer to help move the case through court. Both the executor and the lawyer are entitled to fees that can be based on the dollar value of the probated estate.

If your Will doesn't name a friendly executor, the court can appoint anyone to do the job and can determine how much that person should be paid. In some jurisdictions, there are concerns that the court appoints cronies who, in turn, financially support the judge's political party.

What does this have to do with Savings Bonds?

Some types of property, including Savings Bonds, can pass to heirs outside of your Will and Probate Court. These types of property have a co-owner or beneficiary and, besides Savings Bonds, include jointly owned accounts, bank accounts registered in-trust-for, life insurance, and IRA, pension, and Keogh accounts.

Savings Bonds with a living co-owner or beneficiary automatically avoid probate.

Savings Bonds with a single owner, on the other hand, go through the probate process and are distributed according to the owner's Will.

Savings Bonds with a co-owner or beneficiary who died *before* the owner are actually sole-owner bonds, even though they have two names on the. They go through probate.

Savings Bonds with a co-owner or beneficiary who died *after* the owner are also sole-owner bonds, but belong to the estate of the co-owner or beneficiary, not to the estate of the owner.

Another option – the Living Trust

Don't confuse a *Living Trust* with a *Living Will*. A Living Will allows you to give someone the power to make health care decisions for you. A Living Trust is used in estate planning as a legal alternative to a Will.

Instead of leaving what you own to your heirs with a Will, you can set up a Living Trust and give everything you own to the trust before you die. The Living Trust will have a legal lifetime that extends beyond yours.

Typically when you set up a Living Trust, you name yourself as the trustee who controls the property in the trust. You also designate another person who will become the trustee after your death.

The primary attraction of a Living Trust in estate planning is that, done right, it allows your heirs to avoid the delay, expense, and lack of privacy of Probate Court. This is because you won't own anything when you die – you will have given it all to the Living Trust.

It's possible to have paper Savings Bonds, but not TreasuryDirect's electronic bonds, registered in the name of a Living Trust. Details are in the section of Chapter 12 called *Changing the owner to a trust.*

Problems of Living Trusts

Of course, there will also be legal fees associated with setting up a Living Trust. Moreover, if retitling property to the trust isn't properly completed, all your property ends up in Probate Court anyhow.

The Office of the Attorney General of New York warns: *Contrary to the impression created by many Living Trust sales-people, the grantor must take affirmative steps to transfer assets and fund the trust. Merely executing the Living Trust itself will not cause the trust to become funded.*

Book Note 10-1 links to the New York Attorney General's page on Living Trusts

Consequently, even if you have a Living Trust, you should also have a Will, known as a *pour-over* (to catch what pours over the brim of your Living Trust, I guess), to make sure any property that doesn't get into the trust is distributed as you wish.

Moreover, in terms of privacy, the NY Attorney General's office says: *A "pour-over" becomes a matter of public record when it is submitted for probate, and the "pour-over" often incorporates the Living Trust by reference. In addition, when title to real property is transferred into a Living Trust as part of the funding process, the consent of the mortgagee is required. Before giving consent to the transfer of mortgaged property, the mortgagee typically requires that the Living Trust document be recorded, with the deed, at the office of the county clerk. The Living Trust can then become part of the publicly-accessible records.*

Minimizing taxes when passing on Savings Bonds

There are two kinds of tax issues that you have to consider when passing Savings Bonds to heirs – income taxes and estate taxes.

Income tax issues

In Chapter 14 we'll look in depth at the tax-deferral feature of Savings Bonds. For this chapter you just need to remember that in addition to passing on your investment in Savings Bonds, you may also be passing on a significant amount of unpaid income taxes.

Property that changes in value, such as a company's stock, receives a *stepped-up basis* when it is inherited. This frees the heir from paying capital gains taxes on any increase in the property's value that occurred during your lifetime. Savings Bonds, however, don't have capital gains, they earn tax-deferred interest, and they don't receive a stepped-up basis.

As we'll discuss in detail in Chapter 11, unless you're declaring the income your bonds earn each year, the executor of your estate has the option of either passing your Savings Bonds on without paying the tax or putting all the interest earned up to the date of your death on your final tax return.

This can make sense if you're in a lower tax bracket than your heirs and the lump of Savings Bond income doesn't put you in a higher tax bracket.

However, this will also set the *double-taxation trap*, which is discussed in Chapter 17, and end the yield-boosting advantages of tax-deferral.

Likewise, if you are in a low tax bracket now, it can make sense for you to redeem Savings Bonds as part of your estate planning process before your death. Pay the tax on the deferred interest and reinvest.

In particular, you should cash stinker bonds – Savings Bonds that have stopped earning interest – and get the tax taken care of.

Now for a bit of good news – Savings Bond interest is exempt from state and local income taxes.

Estate tax issues

Now for a bit of bad news – the value of your Savings Bonds is not exempt from estate taxes at either the state or federal level. This is the case even if you pass on your Savings Bonds using a co-owner or beneficiary designation.

The co-owner and beneficiary designations avoid probate, but they don't avoid estate taxes. The same is true for Living Trusts. The NY Attorney General's office warns:

There is no inherent estate tax advantage to using a Living Trust. While a trust may contain provisions taking effect at death which do save on taxes, the identical tax savings can be contained in the grantor's Will instead of a Living Trust.

For federal estate taxes, in 2006, 2007, and 2008, your executor doesn't even have to file a federal estate tax return if your estate is worth less than $2 million. However, many states have estate taxes that begin at much lower levels, sometimes less than $50,000.

Because estate tax rules vary from state to state, you'll need to consult an advisor in your area to figure out how to minimize the estate tax. In some cases it may require having your Savings Bonds pass through your Will or a Living Trust rather than through a co-owner or beneficiary registration.

If you are near the estate tax threshold in your state, keep in mind that you can redeem your Savings Bonds, pay the income tax, and reinvest what's left. This will lower the value of your estate by the amount of the taxes. It doesn't make sense to pay estate taxes on the part of your Saving Bonds' value that's deferred taxes. Your heirs won't get to keep the money and their tax bracket may be higher than yours anyhow.

Heirs who receive Savings Bonds on which federal estate taxes have been paid can take a deduction for the estate taxes when they pay the income tax on the bonds.

Co-owner / beneficiary pros and cons

Although passing Savings Bonds using a co-owner or beneficiary registration has the advantage of avoiding probate, it can also have disadvantages in some situations.

For example, if your Will states that you want to divide your possessions between two children evenly, but half of your estate is in Savings Bonds and you've made one child the beneficiary on all of them because you want that child to be the executor of your estate, that child can legally keep all your Savings Bonds and one-half of the rest of your estate. Your other child could receive much less than you intended.

There are two additional problems to consider.

The estate tax problem

Say you have two children – Molly and Pete – and half your estate is in Savings Bonds. You make Molly the beneficiary of all your Savings Bonds and distribute the rest of your property to Pete through your Will.

Estate taxes are levied based on the property you owned when you died – including the Savings Bonds. But they are paid with the money that's left in your estate – in this case, with Pete's money.

Because the Savings Bonds were passed using the registration, the estate no longer has the right to cash them. So Pete ends up paying the estate tax on Molly's inheritance.

Assuming Molly loves her brother more than money, she may offer to reimburse Pete for her share of the estate taxes. But when Molly cashes some of the Savings Bonds to pay Pete, she gets stuck with the income tax on the tax-deferred interest the Savings Bonds have earned. Now Molly is coming out on the short end of the stick.

In the best of situations these problems can be solved, but the death of a parent is not the best of situations. Financial problems like these can unintentionally wreak havoc on stressed family relationships.

The even-steven problem

To avoid the estate tax problem, you could change things around and split your Savings Bonds into two groups. Make Molly the co-owner or beneficiary on half and Pete on the other half.

But wait. Each of your bonds has a different value and interest rate. You can't do this fairly just by splitting the bonds up by face value. The older bonds are worth more.

In fact, the only fair way to do this is to have each bond split into two smaller but identical bonds, with Molly the co-owner or beneficiary on one and Pete the co-owner or beneficiary on the other. You can do this as part of the re-registration process described in Chapter 12.

However, depending on the number of ways you want to split your bonds and the available denominations, it may not be possible to accomplish a split. For example, a $500 bond can be split two ways, but not three ways or four ways because there are no smaller denominations that allow that.

In situations like these it may be better to hold your Savings Bonds with a sole-owner registration and to pass them to your heirs through your Will.

Other estate planning issues

Stinker bond issues

Estates have much less flexibility with Savings Bonds that have stopped earning interest. The Treasury won't change the registration on stinker bonds, which means they can't be reissued in the names of your heirs.

Your executor will either cash them, pay all the income tax due on your final return, or pass them to your heirs, who will be forced to cash them and pay the income tax on their returns.

If you own a large investment in Savings Bonds, that big lump of stinker bond interest could put you in the highest tax bracket of your life and you won't even be there to see it!

Moreover, look what can happen if your executor passes the stinker bonds on to your heirs uncashed. Stinker bonds are typically 80% to 90% interest. If your stinker bonds have a redemption value of $100,000, that's how they'll be valued for estate taxes.

Next your heirs cash the bonds, but they have to pay income tax on the interest – which comes to about $20,000 if they're in the 25% tax bracket. So the bonds are actually worth $80,000 to your heirs, but they've just paid estate taxes on $100,000!

The income tax will be paid eventually by someone, so there's no advantage to holding on to these bonds. Give your heirs the gift of redeeming your Savings Bonds as they mature, paying your taxes, and rolling what's left into new Savings Bonds.

Gift tax issues

If you give someone more than $11,000 a year, you may have to file a Form 709 with the IRS for that year, even though you won't actually owe any gift tax until you've given away a lot of money.

If you give a Savings Bond to someone else by having the registration changed to make the other person the owner:

★ you create an income-taxable event for yourself
★ you create a double-taxation trap for the person you're giving the bond to
★ as we just saw with the estate tax, for gift tax purposes your gift is larger than what the recipient will receive after he or she pays the income taxes that are owed on the interest

It's better to redeem the bond, pay the taxes, and give the amount remaining as your gift.

You can add a co-owner or beneficiary to a Savings Bond without creating gift tax issues. However, you are still the primary owner of the Savings Bond and you are responsible for the income tax. That's why these registration changes aren't considered gifts.

When a co-owner redeems a paper EE or I series Savings Bond, the 1099-INT tax form is issued in the co-owner's social security number, but the IRS says it's still the primary owner that owes the tax.

Co-owners should report the income on their tax returns using Schedule B. At the bottom of the interest section they should enter *Nominee distribution* and the name and Social Security Number of the person who actually owes the tax. Then they should use that line to subtract the interest back out of their own interest income. The primary owner would then report it on his or her return.

Make sure your heirs know you own Savings Bonds

It is essential that your heirs and executor know that you own Savings Bonds and can easily find them. Over 5% of all Savings Bonds have stopped earning interest and have never been cashed. In many cases the owners have died and the heirs didn't know to look for them.

Chapter 11

Inheriting Savings Bonds

Finding a decedent's Savings Bonds

Who inherits the bonds?

Tax issues when inheriting Savings Bonds

Redemption or reissue?

The redemption / reissue process

Finding a decedent's Savings Bonds

When someone close to you dies – particularly if you are executor of the estate – it's essential to determine whether the person who died owned any Savings Bonds. You should look for paper bonds in safe deposit boxes, file cabinets, and other locations where the decedent kept financial records.

Remember that over 5% of all Savings Bonds outstanding have stopped earning interest but have never been cashed. In many cases, this is because the heirs who should have received the bonds didn't know about them and didn't look for them.

Some people hide their valuables in unusual places where you're unlikely to find them. So in addition to actual Savings Bonds, you should look for documents that list Savings Bond holdings and documents related to a TreasuryDirect account.

But the safest thing to do is to ask the Treasury for a list of the decedent's Savings Bonds. The process for this and the address to send your letter to is in the first section of Chapter 13, *Finding forgotten Savings Bonds*. Since you're asking for someone who had died, you'll need to provide a death certificate and evidence that you're entitled to receive this information, such as court documentation that identifies you as the estate's Executor.

If you find a TreasuryDirect account number, contact the Treasury regarding the death of the account owner. It will work with you to have the account's assets transferred to the new owner. Details about how to contact the Treasury are in the Appendix.

You should also enter the decedent's Social Security Number in *Treasury Hunt* (see Chapter 13).

Who inherits the bonds?

On the bonds you do find, carefully check the name on the bonds. If the decedent's name is the only name on the bond, the bonds pass to the decedent's estate and are distributed according to the decedent's Will.

On the other hand, if there are two names on the bond, look to see if the names are separated by OR or by POD. If the second person has also died, the bonds go to the estate of the person who died last.

★ the OR separator means that the second person is co-owner of the bonds and now has exclusive rights to them. A co-owner can redeem the bonds without a death certificate.

★ the POD (payable on death) separator means that the second person is the beneficiary of the bonds. To redeem the bonds, the beneficiary must provide the death certificate of the bond's primary owner.

Tax issues when inheriting Savings Bonds

Whether you inherit Savings Bonds through a Will or because you are named as the co-owner or beneficiary, there are tax issues that you need to be aware of.

Income tax issues

As explained in Chapter 14, Savings Bonds are a tax-deferred investment. This means that it's unlikely that income tax has been paid on the interest you're inheritance has earned.

Someone will have to pay the income tax on the interest earned by the bonds. Another way to think of it is that the bonds you're inheriting are worth less than they appear to be. How much less depends on how much tax you or your benefactor's estate has to pay.

When you inherit stocks, mutual funds, and other investments that can change in price, U.S. tax law gives you a *stepped-up basis* on the investments. This means that you will owe capital gains tax on any price increases only from the day your benefactor died, not from the day your benefactor bought the investment. The capital gains that occurred during your benefactor's life-time are tax-free.

Savings Bonds, however, don't change in price – they earn interest. Savings Bonds don't have capital gains. Likewise, Savings Bonds don't receive a stepped-up basis.

Whether ownership of your benefactor's bonds transfers to you through a co-owner or beneficiary registration or through a Will, the executor of your benefactor's estate has a choice.

The estate can pass the deferred income taxes on to you with the bonds or it can pay the deferred income taxes on the interest earned by the bonds, through the date of your benefactor's death, on your benefactor's final tax return.

The only exception to this is if your benefactor has been paying income tax on the interest each year, rather than letting it defer. In that case the interest up to the time of your benefactor's death must be included on his or her final return.

An executor should consider several factors when making this decision:
* if the decedent is in a lower tax bracket than the heirs, it can be best to declare all the income on the decedent's final return, at the decedent's low tax rate
* likewise, if the estate is over the threshold for estate taxes, it can be best to declare all the income on the decedent's final return. This will lower the value of the estate by the amount of the tax paid
* however, if declaring the lump of deferred interest on the decedent's final return pushes the decedent into a higher tax bracket than the heirs, it can be best to pass the deferred taxes on to the heirs

Use the tax rates in Table 14-1 to determine who has the lower tax rate.

But keep in mind that if the executor does pay the tax on the decedent's final return, this sets the double-taxation trap for the heirs (see Chapter 17). They could end up accidentally paying the income tax a second time!

If your benefactor's executor decides to pay the tax, ask the executor to provide you with a copy of your benefactor's final tax return as proof that the taxes have been paid. Without this proof, the IRS will assume the taxes haven't been paid.

Of course, in this case, you also have to remember when you redeem the bonds that part of the tax you owe has already been paid. Typically this detail is forgotten and you get snared in the double-taxation trap.

Estate tax issues

In addition to income taxes, the decedent's estate may also owe federal or state estate taxes. If estate taxes are owed, the value of all of the decedent's Savings Bonds – no matter if the registration included a co-owner or a beneficiary or not – are included in the estate.

Although estates with a total value of less than $2 million aren't currently required to even file a Federal estate tax return, the same isn't necessarily true for your state's estate taxes. Some states collect estate taxes on estates as small as $50,000.

When you inherit Savings Bonds through a co-owner or beneficiary designation, an unusual situation occurs. The estate can owe tax on the value of the Savings Bonds, but doesn't get any of the Savings Bond money to pay the taxes with. Don't be surprised if the heirs who don't receive Savings Bonds ask you to share in the estate-tax expense.

If the estate does pay Federal estate taxes, make sure you get IRS-acceptable documentation from the executor of the estate regarding how much estate tax was paid on the Savings Bonds.

In the year that you cash a bond and report the interest, you can claim a deduction for any federal estate tax that was paid on the interest portion of a Savings Bond's value.

Redemption or reissue?

No matter who will pay the tax, you also have to decide whether to redeem the bonds you've inherited or to keep them.

Keeping them involves having the bonds reissued so that they are registered in your name.

However, reissue isn't an option for Savings Bonds that have stopped earning interest or are within a month of doing so. These bonds must be redeemed.

Otherwise, to determine whether to redeem the bonds or have them reissued, there are two primary things you have to consider:

★ how will cashing them impact your income taxes?

★ can you get a better return on the money elsewhere at a level of risk you're comfortable with?

In order to determine the income-tax impact of cashing the bonds, you need to know:

★ how much of the value of the bond is deferred interest

★ your current tax rate (see the first section of Chapter 14)

★ are the Savings Bonds old enough to be earning a significant tax-deferred yield (see *Yield of tax deferment* in Chapter 14)

When you cash a bond, you'll receive a 1099-INT tax form for that year reporting all the interest the bond has earned. The IRS will also get a copy.

The fact that the interest was earned while the person who bequeathed the bonds to you was alive makes no difference. Unless your benefactor paid the interest each year and left you proof that the taxes have been paid, the IRS will expect you to pay the income tax, at your rates, on the entire amount of deferred interest.

Consequently, when you inherit a large amount of Savings Bonds, it often makes sense from a tax perspective to cash them over a period of several years. If you cash them all in one year, the total of the deferred interest income could push you into a higher tax bracket or cause other tax problems.

In order to determine whether you can get a better return, you'll have to determine:

★   the Savings Bond interest rates currently being earned

★   the amount of risk you find acceptable

As you can see elsewhere in this book, depending on the series and issue date, Savings Bonds pay a variety of interest rates. Some are above the general level of interest rates being paid by alternative low-risk investments, but others Savings Bonds pay less.

If you are willing to take on more risk, you may be able to get a better return than Savings Bonds over long terms, but there are no guarantees.

In any case, make sure you understand the hidden interest rate penalty discussed in Chapter 16 before you redeem any Savings Bonds you inherit.

•

The redemption / reissue process

When there is a living co-owner or beneficiary

When a registrant listed on a Savings Bond dies, the surviving registrant can redeem the bond in the usual way. Take your personal identification and, if you are the beneficiary, a certified copy of the bond owner's death certificate.

If you would prefer to keep the bond, you can update the registration by submitting the following form. The form includes complete instructions.

Send a certified copy of the death certificate of the bond's owner with your request. You can make yourself the bond's sole owner or you can add a co-owner or beneficiary.

★ **Public Debt Form 4000**, *Request to Reissue United States Savings Bonds.*

See Book Note 11-1

If you don't have internet access, you can order a copy of this form by mail. See the Appendix for complete instructions.

When all bond registrants have died

When all bond registrants have died, things get a bit more complicated. The exact process for redeeming or re-issuing the decedent's Savings Bonds depends on whether the estate:
   ★ is currently being handled by a probate court
   ★ was handled by a probate court but the case is closed
   ★ is being settled under state small estate law
   ★ is being settled with no court involvement

Later in this section you'll find the exact process for each case (the second and third cases use the same process).

In each case, the executor of the estate or the heir must take one or more forms to a bank to have his or her signature certified on the form.

In general, if the bonds are to be redeemed, the back of the bonds should also be signed and certified. If the bonds are to be reissued, on the other hand, the back of the bonds should be left blank.

Required documentation

When all bond registrants have died, reissue and redemption requests require:

★ proof of death for everyone named on the bond

★ proof of the identity of the person making the request, and

★ evidence that the person making the request is entitled to make the request

  ★ if the estate is open and being administered by a court, documentation - no more than a year old - that the court has appointed the person making the request as the estate's representative

  ★ otherwise, a certified copy of the decree of distribution, the final account, a small estates affidavit, an agreement among entitled parties, or other appropriate documentation as described below

Acceptable proof of death is a copy of a death certificate that is certified to be true and correct and that includes the visible seal of the certifying authority. Newspaper or funeral home notices are not acceptable proof of death.

Incapacitated owners and executors

If an executor is asking for redemption or reissue or if any of the heirs have a legal disability, such as being a minor or incompetent, the signer will need to use one of the following forms to furnish proof of authority:

★ If the representative has been appointed by a court use **Public Debt Form 1455**, *Request by Fiduciary for Reissue or Distribution of United States Savings Bonds* (this form is the one for executors)

See Book Note 11-2

★ Otherwise, use **Public Debt Form 2513**, *Application by Voluntary Guardian of Incapacitated Owner of United States Bonds or Notes*

See Book Note 11-3

Estate handled with Court Administration

Redemption – A court-appointed representative of a deceased person's estate can redeem some or all of the estate's Savings Bonds by taking the bonds to a financial institution, along with all of the required documentation mentioned earlier, and requesting payment.

The representative will have to sign the back of the bonds in the presence of a bank official and show his or her fiduciary capacity – for example, *John Doe, executor of the will of Mary Doe, deceased.*

The financial institution may cash the bonds immediately but is not obligated to do so. At a minimum, the financial institution will certify the representative's signature on the back of the bonds. See the Appendix for the address of a Federal Reserve Savings Bond processing center where the bonds and all required documentation to request payment can be sent.

If there are a large number of bonds and a list including serial numbers is readily available, the representative can avoid having to sign all the bonds by having his or her signature certified on **Public Debt Form 1522**, *Special Form for Request of Payment of United States Savings and Retirement Securities Where Use of a Detached Request is Authorized.*

See Book Note 11-4

Reissue – A court-appointed representative of the deceased person's estate can have some or all of the estate's Savings Bonds reissued by submitting all required documentation mentioned earlier plus – for each person entitled to the estate's Savings Bonds – a copy of **Public Debt Form 1455**, *Request by Fiduciary for Reissue or Distribution of United States Savings Bonds or Notes.*

See Book Note 11-2

The representative must have a bank officer certify his or her signature on each form. When signing the forms (there's no need for the representative to sign the bonds), the representative should show the fiduciary capacity – for example, *John Doe, executor under the will of Mary Doe, deceased.*

For each copy of Form 1455, if the person inheriting the bonds wants to add a co-owner or beneficiary, also submit a copy of **Public Debt Form 4000**.

See Book Note 11-1

Form 1455 can be used to request redemption as well as reissue, which the representative will find useful if there are multiple heirs, some of whom want the bonds redeemed and some of whom want the bonds reissued.

Heirs who want bonds redeemed should sign the back of the bonds and have their signatures certified by a bank officer before the court-appointed representative sends them in with Form 1455.

Estate is closed or settled under state small estate law

If the estate is closed or if the estate was settled under special provisions of a state law relating to small estates (for example, Summary Administration, Small Estates Act, Texas Muniment of Title, Louisiana Judgment of Possession) then what you need to do depends on whether the settlement awarded specific bonds to specific people on not.

Specific bonds awarded to specific people – Each heir can request payment by taking the required documentation mentioned earlier and some or all of his or her bonds to a financial institution and requesting payment.

These heirs can request reissue of some or all of their bonds by sending the required documentation mentioned earlier and the bonds to the Treasury with a copy of **Public Debt Form 4000**.

See Book Note 11-1

Bond awards not specified – If the court did not award specific bonds to specific people, submit the required documentation mentioned earlier, the bonds, and one copy of **Public Debt Form 5394**, *Agreement and Request for Disposition of a Decedent's Treasury Securities*, with the certified signature and disposition instructions of each heir. The form allows each heir the choice

See Book Note 11-5

of redemption, reissue, both, or transfer of electronic bonds to a TreasuryDirect account.

No court involvement

If the current redemption value of the bonds is more than $100,000, the bonds cannot be distributed without court involvement. Contact a lawyer who handles estates.

Otherwise, Federal law provides that Savings Bonds belonging to an estate being settled without administration must be distributed in a specific order of precedence.

For example, if there is a surviving spouse and no surviving child, the bonds go to the spouse.

If there is a surviving spouse and surviving children or descendents of children, one half to the spouse and one half to the others.

And so on.

The complete and detailed order of precedence is in the instructions to **Public Debt Form 5336**, *Disposition of Securities Belonging to a Decedent's Estate Being Settled without Administration.*

See Book Note 11-6

The person or persons highest in the order of precedence should submit the required documentation mentioned earlier and the bonds with the form. The form allows each heir the choice of redemption, reissue, both, or transfer of electronic bonds to a TreasuryDirect account.

Chapter 12

Changing the registration

Why change the registration?

Registration, death, and taxes

Changing the owner to a trust

Changing the registration in TreasuryDirect

Changing the registration on paper Savings Bonds

Why change the registration?

In Chapter 5, I discussed Savings Bond registration from the point of view of someone making an investment in Savings Bonds.

That chapter has basic information about Savings Bonds registration that you'll need before attacking this chapter. It includes a discussion of why you might want to register Savings Bonds one way or another for estate planning purposes and Chapter 10 expands on that information.

For an overview of information about Savings Bond registrations, see Chapter 5.

There are some situations in which the Treasury will refuse to change the registration. For example, the registration on bonds that have stopped paying interest can't be changed. In fact, the Treasury won't even change the registration when the bond is in its final month of paying interest.

The Treasury won't reissue bonds to fix minor spelling errors if the registration information is sufficient to establish ownership.

Neither will it split a large bond into smaller denominations (unless the new bonds have different registrations – for example, different co-owners), although you can accomplish something similar by initiating a partial redemption of a large bond.

Neither the delivery address, which may include a name, nor the Social Security Number can be changed. Neither represents a right to the bond. The delivery address is simply where the Treasury mailed the paper bond when it was issued. Like the SSN, it's only used to track lost bonds, not for redemption or tax purposes.

The Treasury says you don't need to have a bond reissued to update a name changed by marriage, but the forms will allow you to do so.

To update a registration because of a name change or to fix a significant error in the original registration, use the same form as for changing a beneficiary, which we'll get to in a moment here.

When you send bonds in to have the registration changed there's no need to sign the back of the bonds. In fact, signing the back of the bonds is a signal to the Treasury that you want redemption, not reissue, so things can get confused if you sign bonds you want reissued.

Registration, death, and taxes

Changing a registrant who has died

If you want to change a Savings Bond's registration because the **owner** has died, the information you need is in Chapter 11, *Inheriting Savings Bonds*.

To change a **co-owner** or **beneficiary** who has died, on the other hand, follow the instructions in this chapter. In some of these cases, the signature of the co-owner or beneficiary is required. In those cases you should include a certified copy of the registrant's death certificate when you submit the request to have the registration changed.

Creating a taxable event

There are a few registration changes that create a taxable event. A taxable event causes a 1099-INT tax form to be issued to the IRS and the original owner, forcing income tax to be paid on the bond's earnings as of the date of the change, as if the bond was redeemed.

If a registration change is going to create a taxable event anyhow, seriously consider just cashing in the old bond and buying a new one with the registration you want. This simplifies the transaction and avoids the double-taxation trap discussed in Chapter 17.

Adding or changing the non-principal co-owner or the beneficiary doesn't create a taxable event. Changing a living principal owner, on the other hand, always creates a taxable event, except in a few special cases we'll get to in a moment.

The redemption-repurchase route to changing the registration on your Savings Bonds has the following advantages and disadvantages:

★ Advantages:
  ★ no forms to fill out
  ★ provides an opportunity to switch from one series to another, from paper bonds to TreasuryDirect, or to change denominations
  ★ restarts the 30-year maturity clock
  ★ no limitations on whose name can be on the new bond
  ★ if reissue would create a taxable event, redemption-repurchase avoids the *Double-Taxation Trap* (see Chapter 17)
  ★ if the new owner has a higher tax rate than the current owner, it's better to create a taxable event and pay income tax at the current owner's lower rate
  ★ new bonds sometimes pay higher interest rates than older bonds

★ Disadvantages:
  ★ if the bonds are H or HH bonds, you won't be able to get a replacement in that series
  ★ if Series EE or I bonds are less than one year old, you can't redeem them
  ★ if Series EE or I bonds are less than five years old, there's a three-month interest penalty on redemption
  ★ the $30,000 maximum annual purchase limit could prevent repurchase of a large amount of Savings Bonds
  ★ older bonds often pay higher interest rates than new bonds
  ★ redemption-repurchase will always create a taxable event for the original owner and end any ongoing advantages of tax deferral

Changing the owner to a trust

Before we look at more typical registration changes, let's discuss changing a Savings Bond registration to make a trust the owner of your bond. There's more information on why you might want to do this in Chapter 10.

New paper Savings Bonds can be registered in the name of a trust and old paper Savings Bonds can be reissued to change the registration to a trust. TreasuryDirect's electronic Savings Bonds, on the other hand, can only be registered in the name of a natural person, not a trust. This may change in the future.

The form for requesting reissue to a trust is **Public Debt Form 1851**, *Request to Reissue United States Savings Bonds to a Personal Trust.*

When you complete this form, you are required to check one of two boxes that basically ask whether the trust will provide you a way to get out of paying the tax on the bonds.

If the trust treats you in a way that will force you to pay the tax on the Savings Bond interest when the bonds are redeemed, you can have the bonds reissued without creating a taxable event.

Otherwise you have to check the other box, in which case you'll receive by return mail the reissued bond and a 1099-INT for the interest earned to date. If changing the registration is going to cause a taxable event anyhow, you should consider the option of cashing in your old bonds and buying new ones in the name of the trust.

The instructions on the form go into detail about what provisions are related to each kind of trust. It also has an IRS address you can write to for a ruling if you still have a question about a particular kind of trust after reading the information in the form's instructions.

If your trust has two trustees and either can act for the trust, make sure the word *OR* appears between the names of the trustees in the Savings Bond registration. In that case either trustee will be able to act for the trust in Savings Bond transactions.

See Book Note 12-1.

If you don't have internet access, you can order a copy of this form by mail. See the Appendix for complete instructions.

Changing the registration in TreasuryDirect

There are three different ways to change the registration in TreasuryDirect.

★ add, remove, or change the co-owner or beneficiary associated with a bond

★ move a bond to your *Gift Box* in someone else's name

★ transfer the bond to someone else's TreasuryDirect account

The first option, adding, removing, or changing a co-owner or beneficiary – is never a taxable event in TreasuryDirect. However the other two options change the owner and therefore are taxable events. Proceed with caution – especially if you receive a message that your transaction may be taxable.

Most registration changes are easily handled using the first method. Log into your TreasuryDirect account and click the *Manage Direct* tab in the row of buttons across the top of the screen.

On the page that appears, the first section of links is called *Manage My Account*. One of the links in that section is called *Update my Registration List*. Use that link to add the new registration to your list of registrations.

Note that each registration can have one or two registrants, but each must be an individual with a Social Security Number (for paper Savings Bonds, other registration options are available).

You can create registrations with or without your own name on the bonds. To create registrations without yourself as the first-named registrant, you have to check the box marked *This is a gift*.

Once you have the registration the way you want it in your list of registrations, return to the *Manage Direct* page and find the section of links called *Manage My Securities*. In that section, select the link, *Edit a registration*.

Next you will be asked to select the Savings Bond you want to change the registration for. A page describing that bond will appear along with a drop-down that will display your registration list. The bond's current registration will be selected. Change it to the one you really want and click the *Add New Registration* button.

If the registration you select names someone besides you as the first-named owner, the bond will be moved to your *Gift Box*, which is an area inside your own TreasuryDirect account. Don't forget this is a taxable transaction.

To transfer a Savings Bond to someone else's TreasuryDirect account, the new owner has to actually have a TreasuryDirect account. It seems obvious, but sometimes people miss that detail. This time, click on the *Manage Direct* button, find the section called *Manage My Securities* and click on *Transfer Securities*.

On the pages that follow, you will first select the bond you want to transfer, then you'll be able to specify who you want to transfer the bond to. You will need both the recipient's Social Security Number and TreasuryDirect Account Number.

Bonds can be transferred from either your regular bonds or from your *Gift Box*. Bonds in your *Gift Box* must be transferred to the actual owner before they can be redeemed.

Like moving a bond to your *Gift Box*, transferring a bond to someone else is an ownership transfer that will create a taxable event for you – you'll owe income tax on the interest earned by the bond up to the date of the transfer.

Adding, removing, or changing the co-owner or beneficiary in TreasuryDirect, on the other hand is never a taxable event. Moreover, in TreasuryDirect these changes never require the permission of the co-owner or beneficiary, as they do in most situations with paper Savings Bonds.

Changing the registration on paper Savings Bonds

If you want to change a registration because one of the registrants has died, begin by reviewing the *Registration, death, and taxes* section earlier in this chapter. That section includes additional information on what you'll need to submit with your change request that isn't repeated here.

First we'll look at the form used to change a Savings Bond's registration, then at the rules.

Form

You can download this form or obtain paper copies using the instructions in the Appendix. The form includes its own instructions. You'll find the mailing address for your request in those instructions.

You are required to have your signature certified on the form by a bank. Do not sign the back of the bonds themselves but do include them in the package when you submit your request.

All registration change requests now use **Public Debt Form 4000** – *Request to Reissue United States Savings Bonds.*

In the past there have been special forms for changing owners and co-owners and for make changes to Series I bond registrations, however, those forms have been discontinued.

If you don't have internet access, you can order a copy of this form by mail. See the Appendix for complete instructions.

If you do have internet access, go to our web site and click on Book Note 12-2.

Changing a living owner or principal co-owner

Changing a sole owner or a principal co-owner is a taxable event except in a few specific situations.

Changing or removing a non-principal co-owner isn't a taxable event, however, you have to proceed carefully because:

★ The IRS considers the principal co-owner to be:
  ★ the person who put up the funds to buy the bond, or
  ★ the person who received the bond as a gift or inheritance

★ But unless you specify otherwise, the Treasury considers the principal co-owner to be:
  ★ the first person named in the Savings Bond registration.

Thus if the second-named co-owner is the person who actually put up the money to buy the bond or who received it as a gift or inheritance, you have to tell the Treasury that. If you don't, the Treasury will process the change as a taxable transaction and you and the IRS will receive a 1099-INT tax form reporting the interest the bond has earned so far.

If two people go together to invest in a bond, then each is considered to be the principal co-owner to the extent of his or her share of the investment. This split also applies for estate-tax purposes.

There are a few exceptions to the rule that changing the sole or principal co-owner is a taxable event. These exceptions include:

★ Death of the sole owner or co-owner.
★ Removing or changing a co-owner who didn't put up any of the money used to buy the bond.
★ Transferring bonds between spouses or as part of a divorce, except in community property states.
★ Having bonds that you and a co-owner bought jointly reissued to each of you separately in the same proportion as your contribution to the purchase price.
★ Transferring bonds to a trust, but only when you are considered the owner of the trust and the increase in value both before and after the transfer continues to be taxable to you.

For official documentation on these exceptions, see IRS Publication 550, *Investment Income and Expenses*.

See Book Note 12-3

Unless you are eligible for one of the taxable-event exceptions, changing the sole owner or principal co-owner will set you up for the *double-taxation trap* (see Chapter 17). To avoid this trap, make sure you record the serial number of each bond, put the serial number on your tax form when you pay the tax, and give the new owner a copy of that tax return as proof that you've already paid some of the tax on the bond.

Read the Tax Liability section on the third page of the form carefully. If you are eligible for an exception to the creation of a taxable event, include a separate letter with the form explaining why.

Any new owner or co-owner must be a natural person – in particular, it can't be a charitable organization. Except in the cases of the death of the registrant or a court order related to a divorce:

★ changing or removing an owner or co-owner requires the signatures of both the owner and co-owner

★ the new owner or co-owner must be related to you by blood or marriage or be a trust that benefits you or an eligible person.

Co-owner and beneficiary additions, deletions, or changes

Changing or removing a non-principal co-owner or a beneficiary isn't a taxable event.

However, changing or removing the co-owner on any paper Savings Bond, as well as changing the beneficiary on the older and no longer issued Series E or Series H bonds, requires the consent of the current co-owner or beneficiary.

To avoid processing delays, make sure both the owner and the co-owner or beneficiary have their signatures certified on the required form by a bank.

Also:

★ keep in mind that a Savings Bond registration can have only a co-owner or a beneficiary, not both; among other changes, you can use the form to remove a co-owner and add a beneficiary or to remove a beneficiary and add a co-owner

★ both co-owners and beneficiaries must be natural persons; legal entities such as trusts or charitable organizations can't be co-owners or beneficiaries

★ as mentioned earlier in the section on TreasuryDirect, the co-owner on electronic Savings Bonds can be changed without the co-owner's signature; with paper bonds the co-owner's signature is required.

Chapter 13

Lost and stolen Savings Bonds

Finding forgotten Savings Bonds

Treasury Hunt

Destroyed, stolen, and lost Savings Bonds

Finding forgotten Savings Bonds

You can confirm that the Savings Bond inventory you created in Chapter 9 includes all of your unredeemed Savings Bonds by asking the Treasury to send you a printout of your bond holdings, including series, issue date, face value, and serial number.

Savings Bonds you have already redeemed will not be on the list. If some of the bonds on the list are indeed lost, I'll tell you how to get them replaced in a minute here.

In your letter, you should provide as much information as you can. At a minimum you must provide your name, current address and your social security number.

But the Treasury's ability to search improves as you provide additional information, such as the approximate issue date of the bonds, the series and denomination, your name and address at the time of issue, and, if the bond was a gift to you, the giver's social security number.

If you have an inventory that includes serial numbers but you're not sure if the bonds have been cashed, also include those serial numbers.

If the owner of the bonds has died and you're the representative of his or her estate, provide documentation of your status and a copy of the death certificate of the owner.

Make sure your request says you want a list of your unredeemed bonds. Sign your request and send it to:

Bureau of the Public Debt
Accrual Securities Branch
P. O. Box 1328
Parkersburg, WV 26106-1328

Treasury Hunt

There's another way to search for bonds that have stopped earning interest or that were returned to the Treasury by the Post Office. It's an online system the Treasury provides called *Treasury Hunt*, which is shown in Figure 13-1.

Although the web pages say TreasuryDirect, you don't have to be a TreasuryDirect account holder to use *Treasury Hunt*.

You enter your Social Security Number (with or without dashes) and click the *Search* button.

Note that for gift bonds, you should also try the SSN of the giver.

You will get a hit if the SSN you enter matches the data on an unredeemed registered Treasury security (both Savings Bonds and marketable Treasury securities are in the system) that:

★ Has stopped earning interest

★ Was returned as undeliverable in 1996 or later (each year, the Post Office returns over 15,000 Savings Bonds and 25,000 interest payments to the Treasury undelivered)

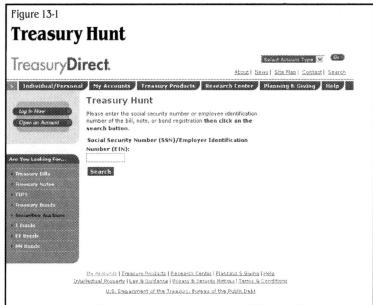

Figure 13-1

It's important to note that the information in *Treasury Hunt* is incomplete.

In particular, it doesn't include older Savings Bonds that didn't have an SSN in the registration record and it doesn't include securities that are still earning interest.

This means it won't find "lost" Savings Bonds if they were delivered correctly and are still earning interest.

Moreover, keep in mind that the SSN on a Savings Bond doesn't necessarily belong to the owner of the bond. When Savings Bonds are bought as gifts, the gift giver has the option to put his or her own SSN on the purchase form rather than the SSN of the actual owner. This is very likely to happen when the gift giver doesn't know the SSN of the recipient.

The SSN on a paper Savings Bond registration is mostly used to track lost bonds, as in *Treasury Hunt*. It's also used by government agencies distributing benefits to ensure that recipients meet asset limits. In TreasuryDirect, but not with paper bonds, it determines who owes tax on Savings Bond interest.

Ready? To get to *Treasury Hunt*, go to our web site, click on Book Note 13-1.

Treasury Hunt? Book Note 13-1

Destroyed, stolen, and lost Savings Bonds

Savings Bonds never received

When you buy a Savings Bond at a bank or through your payroll savings plan, it should arrive within three calendar weeks. If you don't receive the bond by then, contact your bank or payroll office, which will work with the federal office that issues Savings Bonds to find the missing bond or get you a replacement.

They will have you fill out a form you can see at Book Note 13-2

Military safekeeping

The Department of Defense offers a program called military safekeeping to members of the armed services who are on active duty. The program allows the military to hold Savings Bonds purchased through a military payroll savings plan rather than having them mailed to you.

If you participated in a plan like this and you've never claimed your Savings Bonds, the Department of Defense still has them. Book Note 13-3 links to a list of contacts – depending on which branch of the armed forces you were in – that you can use to claim your Savings Bonds.

Military safekeeping – Book Note 13-3

Savings Bonds received, then lost

If you know that a Savings Bond has been lost, stolen, or destroyed, you can have it replaced without a fee. To do so, you'll need a copy **Public Debt Form 1048** – *Claim for lost, stolen, or destroyed United States Savings Bonds.*

Link to this form at Book Note 13-4

You can download a copy of this form from our web site. Click on Book Note 13-4. Start by reading the instructions on the last page of the form, which include the address where you should mail the form after completing it.

If you don't have internet access, you can order a copy of this form by mail. See the Appendix for complete instructions.

You can provide approximate issue dates and you can enter *unknown* for denominations and serial numbers, but you must provide the registration information – the name of the owner and the Social Security Number that appeared on the bond (if the bond was a gift, the address and SSN could be the giver's rather than the bond owner's).

You will have to take the form to a bank and have your signature certified on the form before mailing it in.

The Treasury will find your bonds in its records and make sure that they haven't already been cashed. On the form, you can ask to have the bonds replaced (they'll have the original issue date), or you can ask for the funds.

A claim that a bond was redeemed by someone other than the owner or co-owner requires a higher level of information that may involve police reports or other legal documents. There's more information on dealing with Savings Bond fraud on the last page of Chapter 5.

If you haven't lost your Savings Bonds yet, reading this chapter should give you some incentive to go back to Chapter 9 and create an inventory of your Savings Bonds as soon as you can.

Other lost property? Your state's attorney general has an unclaimed property department. In most states, the records of lost property are searchable over the internet. It's unlikely you'll find a Savings Bond, but you may find other funds that were lost in the mail or otherwise didn't get to you. To search the unclaimed property database of your state, go to our web site, click on Book Note 13-5.

Part III –
Redeeming your investment

Managing the deferred-tax time bomb

Is tax-deferral better than higher rates?

Basics of Savings Bond redemption

How to minimize the income tax bite

Chapter 14

Managing the deferred-tax time bomb

Your marginal tax rate

The tax-deferral feature of Savings Bonds

What is the deferred-tax time bomb?

When your tax rate is headed up, avoid tax deferral

Your marginal tax rate

Before we can discuss the tax-deferral feature of Savings Bonds in the depth it deserves, we have to make sure that you understand what marginal tax rates are and that you know what yours is.

In the United States, income tax rates are graduated. The higher your income, the higher your tax rate. The graduated scales have many fewer steps and lower rates now than they used to, however.

Your top rate is called your *marginal* rate because you pay it only on the part of your income that exceeds the threshold for that rate. In other words, everyone pays the same percentage on lower levels of income – the higher rates apply only to the portion of your income that exceeds the threshold amount for that rate.

This means that when you are in a situation where you can move income from one year to another, you will pay the least in taxes if you move your income to the year in which you are in the lowest tax bracket and have the lowest marginal tax rate.

The tax-deferral feature of Savings Bonds gives you this kind of flexibility. Within the range of the 30-year life of a Savings Bond, you can choose when to redeem the bond and pay the income tax on the interest you've earned. In fact, you don't even have to redeem your bond to pay the accumulated tax, as I'll explain in a minute here.

Our web site includes the values for prior years and is updated when new data becomes available. Click on Book Notes and go to Note 14-1.

Table 14-1 will help you determine your tax bracket or marginal tax rate. You need to know your filing status and your taxable income.

Your taxable income is not the same as your total income, but is your income after deductions and exemptions. Look for the line on your tax return labeled *Taxable Income*.

Table 14-1

2007 US Tax Rates

When your taxable income is over:				Your marginal tax rate is:
Single	Married Joint Return	Married Separate Return	Head of Household	
$0	$0	$0	$0	10%
$7,825	$15,650	$7,825	$11,200	15%
$31,850	$63,700	$31,850	$42,650	25%
$77,100	$128,500	$64,250	$110,100	28%
$160,850	$195,850	$97,925	$178,350	33%
$349,700	$349,700	$174,850	$349,700	35%

The tax-deferral feature of Savings Bonds

Savings Bonds are tax-deferred investments. This means that rather than paying income tax on the interest you earn each year, you don't owe any income tax on the interest until you redeem the bond.

The IRS says this feature is only available to cash-method taxpayers (not accrual-method taxpayers). If you don't know which you are, you're a cash-method taxpayer. The accrual method requires extensive bookkeeping and is usually done only by businesses or other organizations, not by individuals.

While there are benefits to tax-deferred investments, there can be even bigger benefits to earning a higher interest rate to begin with. We have a great example of this in our analysis of 1.5% HH bonds, which we'll tell you about in the next chapter.

Their tax-deferral feature gives Savings Bonds two advantages that standard investments lack.

First, tax-deferral gives you the opportunity to move income into years in which your tax rate is low. Tax-deferred investments are particularly suitable for investors who expect their tax rate to drop near the end of the time they hold the investment.

The second advantage of tax-deferred investments is that rather than giving up part of your interest each year to pay income tax, the Treasury "loans" you the tax amount and lets you earn interest on it. This makes tax-deferred investments like free money.

However, when you look up the redemption value of your Savings Bonds, don't forget that you have to pay back that loan. You get to keep the interest the loan has earned, but not the loan itself. Compared to investments that don't have the benefit of tax-deferral, the *actual value* of a Savings Bond investment is much lower than its *redemption value*.

Moving income to a low tax-rate year

Let's look in more detail at the first advantage of a tax-deferred investment – the ability to move your income into a year with a lower tax rate.

An example of someone who could take advantage of this would be a person who invested in Savings Bonds during high-income years while working and redeemed them in low-income years after retirement.

It can also make tax sense to cash Savings Bonds, rather than other investments, during a year in which your income is low because of a layoff or other circumstances.

Figure 14-1 shows the difference between a Savings Bond's *redemption value* and *actual value*.

The 100% line across the top of the graph is the redemption value. The three declining lines show the actual value after taxes – as a percentage of the redemption value – at different tax rates.

The lines decline as more and more of the bond's value is interest and less is less is your original investment.

For example, at the point at which an EE bond reaches face value, interest makes up 50% of what it's worth. What you originally paid for the bond makes up the other 50%.

For Series EE bonds, the highest this percentage goes is just over 80%. Some Series E bonds paid interest for 40 years; for these the percentage can go as high as just over 90%.

But these are the extremes. The percentage on your own bonds is almost certainly lower.

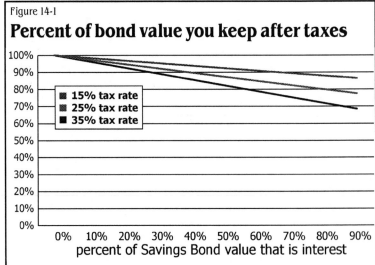

Figure 14-1

Percent of bond value you keep after taxes

■ 15% tax rate
■ 25% tax rate
■ 35% tax rate

percent of Savings Bond value that is interest

In Figure 14-1, the space under the line for your tax rate represents how much of your bond's value you get to keep when you cash in the bond. The IRS gets what's above your tax line.

If your tax rate changes while you hold the bond, you get the bonus represented by the distance between your current tax rate and your new lower tax rate.

This is a benefit that you can only get with a tax-deferred investment like a Savings Bond. With a non-tax-deferred investment, you'd pay tax on the interest year-by-year at your current higher rate.

Yield of tax deferment

Now let's look at the second advantage of tax-deferment. Figure 14-2 compares two investments, both earning a 5% return for someone in the 25% tax bracket. In this case the person's tax rate doesn't change at all.

The taxable investment shown on the lower line doesn't grow as fast because each year's interest is reduced by the income tax on that interest. For the tax-deferred investment, on the other hand, the interest isn't reduced by taxes until redemption in the final year.

Instead, the government essentially loans you the tax amount and lets you earn interest on it. Consequently, as you can see in Figure 14-2, the tax-deferred investment grows faster.

As the years go by, it puts more and more distance between itself and the taxable investment.

Although its value drops dramatically at redemption – because all the tax has to paid at that time – after 30

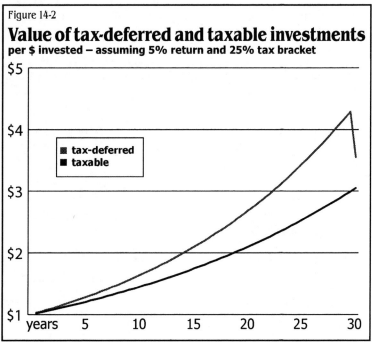

Figure 14-2

Value of tax-deferred and taxable investments
per $ invested – assuming 5% return and 25% tax bracket

- ■ tax-deferred
- ■ taxable

years there's still a remarkable after-tax advantage to the tax-deferred investment.

It's possible to think of this benefit of tax-deferment in terms of additional yield. In other words, when comparing the rates of different investments, you have to add a *tax-deferment yield* onto the interest rate of a tax-deferred investment to determine its total value to you.

As it turns out, the value of the tax-deferment yield depends on three things:
★ the base yield of the investment
★ the length of time you hold the investment
★ your tax rate

Figure 14-3 shows that of these three, the base yield and the time you hold the investment are more important than your tax rate.

The top two lines show the additional tax-deferment yield of a tax-deferred investment with a base yield of 7% – some I bonds have a lifetime yield this high. The level of the top line shows the extra yield for someone in the 35% tax bracket and the next line shows the extra yield for someone in the 15% tax bracket.

After 30 years, tax deferment would add more than 3% to the annual lifetime yield of this investment for a taxpayer in the top tax bracket. In other words, an investment without tax-deferment would require an annual yield of over 10% to match this 7% tax-deferred investment.

The middle two lines in Figure 12-3 show the additional yield from tax deferral for an investment with a 5% base yield. The bottom two lines are for an investment with a 3% base yield.

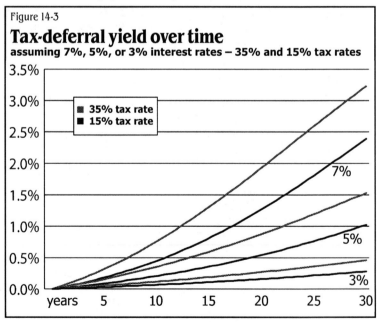

Figure 14-3

Tax-deferral yield over time
assuming 7%, 5%, or 3% interest rates – 35% and 15% tax rates

■ 35% tax rate
■ 15% tax rate

Benefits of tax deferral – summary

The tax-deferral feature of Savings Bonds provides the highest benefits when:
* ★ your Savings Bonds have a high interest rate
* ★ you hold your Savings Bonds for many years
* ★ you are in a high tax bracket
* ★ you expect to be in a lower tax bracket when you redeem your bonds.

If none of these are true, the deferred-tax feature of Savings Bonds is of minimal value to you.

You can keep deferring taxes with Savings Bonds until they reach final maturity and stop paying interest.

Table 14-2 shows how long each series of Savings Bonds pays interest.

Table 14-2

How long Savings Bonds pay interest

Series	First Issued	Last Issued	Years until interest stops	Bonds issued in this year stop paying interest in 2007
E	May 1941	Nov 1965	40	all are stinkers
E	Dec 1965	Jun 1980	30	1977
EE	Jan 1980	---	30	---
I	Sep 1998	---	30	---
H	Jun 1952	Dec 1979	30	1977
HH	Jan 1980	Aug 2004	20	1987

What is the deferred-tax time-bomb?

As wonderful as tax-deferral is, it can blow up on you if you cash in a large Savings Bond investment all at once.

If you have participated in a payroll savings plan or otherwise invested heavily in Savings Bonds, you've made regular, scheduled purchases. To avoid the deferred-tax time bomb, you need to cash them in the same way – on a regular schedule spanning multiple years.

The worst thing you can do is to follow the advice of an unqualified financial consultant who tells you to "just cash them all in."

The reason that cashing them all in is a bad idea is that the boatload of tax-deferred interest you'll receive could push you into a higher tax bracket. It can also increase your income to Alternative Minimum Tax levels or cause you to pay tax on Social Security income you otherwise wouldn't have to pay.

You need to be particularly careful about this if you are near retirement and someone is trying to get you to convert your Savings Bond investment into an annuity. Many people make the mistake of cashing in all their Savings Bonds just before they retire, when they're already in the highest tax bracket of their lives.

The best strategy is to let the bonds quietly earn tax-deferred interest while you're in a high tax bracket, then cash in a few each year after you retire and are in a lower tax bracket. This gives you a do-it-yourself annuity with none of the fees and sales commissions that the let-the-pros-do-it-for-you annuities have.

On the other hand, if all of your Savings Bonds were purchased in the same year or two, they will all mature in the same year or two as well. In this case, you have to plan ahead and start cashing the bonds well before final maturity to spread out the interest income over a multi-year period.

No matter how many bonds you cash, always make sure you hold back enough money to pay the income tax you'll owe on the interest you've earned. How much you'll need to hold back depends on your tax bracket. If it's over several hundred dollars, you may avoid a penalty by sending in an estimated tax payment after you cash your bonds. There's more information on this in Chapter 16.

When your tax rate is headed up, avoid tax deferral

There are two ways to avoid tax deferral. You can either roll over your Savings Bonds or you can ask the IRS to switch from *accrual accounting* (interest is tax-deferred) to *cash accounting* (interest is taxed-as-you-go) for your Savings Bonds.

Savings Bond rollovers

Rolling over a Savings Bond means to redeem an old bond and to buy a new one. Income tax on the interest the old bond has earned will become due in the year you do the rollover. If you are rolling over for tax purposes, you should do it in December. If you hold your bonds in a TreasuryDirect account, it's very easy to do.

However, if your bonds are less than five years old, remember that you pay an early-withdrawal penalty of the most recent three months interest, so you wouldn't want to do it this way every year.

In addition to rolling over Savings Bonds for tax reasons, you may want to roll them over to switch to Series I bonds with a higher fixed base-rate or to switch the May 2005 and later fixed-rate EE bonds to a higher rate.

A rollover is also an easy way to change a Savings Bond's registration. If the registration change is going to be taxable anyhow, it's the best way to do it, because it avoids the *Double-Taxation Trap* (see Chapter 17).

So, the things to remember with rollovers are:
★ you have to pay income tax on the interest the old bonds have earned
★ you will have to pay a three-month interest penalty if your old bonds are less than five years old
★ you are subject to the maximum purchase limits of Savings Bonds (see Chapter 1)

Switching to taxed-as-you-go status

You aren't required to accept the tax-deferral feature of Savings Bonds – the IRS will allow you to pay the income tax on your Savings Bond interest every year.

In general, we don't recommend this because:
* ★ if you select this option, you have to do it for every Savings Bond you own
* ★ thus, if you have a large investment in Savings Bonds, selecting this option will explode the *Deferred-Tax Time-Bomb*
* ★ you are also setting yourself up for the *Double-Taxation Trap* (see Chapter 17)
* ★ you will cancel out the normally advantageous tax-deferral benefit

However, if you are in a much lower tax-bracket now than you expect to be when you cash the bond, it can make sense to pay your tax as you go.

The IRS requirements for switching are minimal – just declare all the interest all of your Savings Bonds have earned on your next tax return. As mentioned, you have to do this for all your bonds – you can't let the interest defer on some bonds and pay-as-you-go on others.

Taking advantage of a child's low tax rate

Consider this example: you buy bonds on a scheduled basis and register them in your child's name. Each year you calculate the interest the bonds have earned and pay income tax at the child's rate.

If your child has more than $1,600 of investment income, including the Savings Bond interest, then the IRS says you have to put income over that amount on your own return until the child turns 18. (Prior to the 2006 tax year, you only had to do this before the child turned 14.)

But given that a Savings Bond investment of even $25,000 won't earn more than $1,600 in one year, you can have the child collect the income and pay the tax. If the child's total income is less than $800, you don't even have to file a tax return for the child.

Your child can pay for college with these bonds – since you have been paying the tax on the interest all along, there's no deferred-tax time-bomb or education deduction to deal with. The tax you pay in the year a bond is cashed will be only on the interest earned that year and should be low to nothing.

But most importantly, you won't have to worry about whether you'll be able to meet any of the many limitations of the regular Savings Bond college education deduction, which are described in Chapter 17. And if your child ends up not going to college, you still receive both your entire investment and the tax benefits.

There's more information on the Savings Bond college education deduction in Chapter 17.

The tricky part of this is remembering from year to year what you're doing. Here's a step-by-step plan:

1. Start buying Savings Bonds in your child's name. Do not include yourself as a co-owner, but you can be a beneficiary.

2. File a tax return for the child. Report all the interest earned so far by all your child's Savings Bonds, including other bonds the child has received as gifts. You won't have a 1099-INT to tell you how much interest to declare, but just calculate how much the bonds are worth in December (see Chapter 8) and subtract the original investment amount. By filing this return you are telling the IRS that you want to switch to the pay-as-you-go, or accrual, method for Savings Bonds. The IRS automatically grants permission for this change.

3. If your child's total income is high enough to require it, continue to file tax returns for your child each year, but now report only the interest the bonds have earned in the current tax year. This amount is the difference in the bond's redemption value from December to December.

4. When you cash the bonds, make sure your child doesn't get caught in the double-taxation trap by paying income tax on the bonds a second time, just because the 1099-INT says to. Instead, on your child's tax return, declare the full amount of interest shown on the 1099, but under it add a line that says *U.S. Savings Bond interest previously reported* and subtract the interest you reported in prior years. It's unlikely that your child would be subject to an IRS audit, but in case that happens hold on to all the tax returns you've filed as proof the taxes have been paid.

You are also allowed to switch back to allowing the interest to defer, although doing so puts the double-taxation trap where you're almost sure to get caught in it.

If you are sure you can keep track of the interest that has been paid, click on Book Note 14-3 to obtain a form that will allow you to switch back. The IRS will automatically grant permission to switch back if you follow the instructions on the form.

Detailed IRS instructions are under the Savings Bond topic of the Interest Income section of IRS Publication 17, Your Federal Income Tax for Individuals. Book Note 14-2 will take you directly to this publication.

Chapter 15

Is tax-deferral better than higher rates?

Why 1.5% Series HH Savings Bonds are a bad choice for almost everyone

Results when your tax rate is steady or goes up

Results when your tax rate goes down

What if you need the current income of Series HH Savings Bonds?

What if you hold 4% Series H / HH Savings Bonds?

Why 1.5% Series HH Savings Bonds are a bad choice for almost everyone

As the Treasury's August 31, 2004 deadline on issuing new Series HH Savings Bonds was approaching, many people exchanged their Series E and EE Savings Bonds for Series HH Savings Bonds who shouldn't have.

Because of the low 1.5% interest rate paid by Series HH Savings Bonds, the conversion only made sense when:

★ The Series E or EE bonds were close to final maturity – that is, they were about to stop paying interest

★ The owner's tax rate would drop after the E or EE bonds had stopped paying interest

If you were among those who made the conversion, you should consider switching to Series I Savings Bonds. Making this switch would mean that you would have to pay income tax on the deferred interest from the Series E or EE bonds you exchanged for the HH bonds.

However, if you can make the switch without exploding the deferred-tax time bomb and if you'd end up with more money, why wouldn't you?

The following analysis applies only to Series H and HH bonds paying 1.5%. There are some that pay 4%; we'll talk more about those later in this chapter.

Figure 15-1 compares two options. Option one is to keep your 1.5% Series HH bond. The alternative option is to redeem the Series HH bond and reinvest the proceeds in a new Series EE or I bond.

To make the comparison equal, we have to assume that under the reinvest in Series EE or I bond option, you would withdraw the same interest amount every six months as the Treasury would have sent you had you invested in Series HH bonds. With TreasuryDirect's electronic bonds, you're allowed to make this kind of partial withdrawal after your electronic bond is a year old.

In the graph, the left-to-right axis indicates how many more years you would hold the bonds.

The front-to-back axis is what proportion of your HH bond's value is deferred interest. For example, if the face value of your HH bond is $500, and the deferred interest entry on the front of the bond says $250, 50% of your HH bond's value is deferred interest.

In the up-and-down axis, zero is in the middle and represents no difference between the two options. The farther the result dips or rises from zero, the better that option is. Positive results favor keeping the 1.5% Series HH Savings Bonds; negative numbers favor switching to Series EE or I bonds. The difference in the two options is calculated at the point at which all bonds have been cashed and all taxes have been paid.

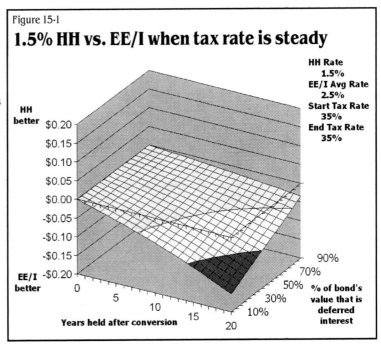

Figure 15-1

1.5% HH vs. EE/I when tax rate is steady

Results when your tax rate is steady or goes up

Figure 15-1, which is repeated on this page, was drawn with the following settings:

★ HH bond rate is 1.5%

★ EE / I bond rate averages 2.5%

★ Income tax rate is the maximum 35% and doesn't change before your final redemption

What the graph clearly shows is that if your tax rate isn't going to change and the Series EE or I bond rate averages at least 2.5%, switching back is always the better option compared to keeping the HH bonds.

The 2.5% Series EE or I bond rate used in the graph was selected to show you the results at an extremely low limit – right now Series EE and I bonds are paying higher rates, which makes this option an even better choice.

If your tax rate isn't going to drop, you should redeem your 1.5% HH bonds (you may need to redeem them over a period of several years to avoid the deferred-tax time bomb discussed in Chapter 14), pay the income tax on the interest you've earned, and reinvest in new Series EE or I bonds. It never makes sense to keep 1.5% Series HH bonds as long as your tax rate is holding steady into the future.

If your tax rate is lower than the maximum 35% shown in the graph, the results hold but the cost of a bad decision is less. If your tax rate goes up, on the other hand, the results hold but the cost of a bad decision is more than what is shown in the graph.

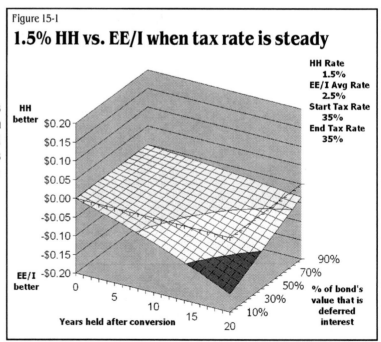

Figure 15-1

1.5% HH vs. EE/I when tax rate is steady

HH Rate
1.5%
EE/I Avg Rate
2.5%
Start Tax Rate
35%
End Tax Rate
35%

HH better

EE/I better

$0.20
$0.15
$0.10
$0.05
$0.00
-$0.05
-$0.10
-$0.15
-$0.20

Years held after conversion

0 5 10 15 20

90%
70%
50%
30%
10%

% of bond's value that is deferred interest

Results when your tax rate goes down

If you're not sure what your income tax rate is and how it will change in the years ahead, now's the time to figure that out. While it's impossible to predict how Congress might change our tax laws in the future, it's easier to predict what your own total income will be.

You can look up your tax rate in our tax rates tables at the beginning of Chapter 14. The table will give you a good idea of where your rate is now and how it might change in the future.

Figure 15-2 was drawn with the following settings:
★   HH bond rate is 1.5%
★   EE / I bond rate averages 2.5%
★   Income tax rate drops to 28% from 35%

In this graph you can see that the feature of Series HH Savings Bonds that allows you to continue to defer taxes until your rate goes down can have a significant impact. Keeping your Series HH bonds is the better choice when your tax rate will go down relatively soon, when the value of your original Series E or EE bonds was primarily interest, and when you expect Series EE/I bonds to pay relatively low interest rates.

Figure 15-3 on the next page is what Figure 15-2 looks like when you view it from the top. From this view it's easier to see the exact curve that separates the two options. The option of keeping HH bonds is better in the upper-left area (dark color); the option of switching back to Series EE/I bonds is better in the lower-left (lighter color) area.

For example, if 50% of the value of your HH bonds was

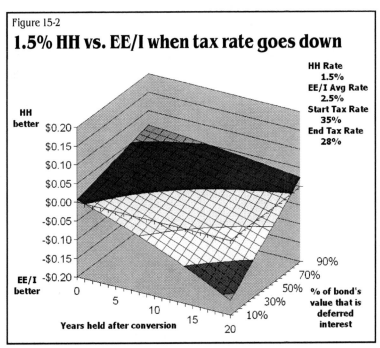

Figure 15-2

1.5% HH vs. EE/I when tax rate goes down

HH Rate
1.5%
EE/I Avg Rate
2.5%
Start Tax Rate
35%
End Tax Rate
28%

HH better

$0.20
$0.15
$0.10
$0.05
$0.00
-$0.05
-$0.10
-$0.15
-$0.20

EE/I better

Years held after conversion

0   5   10   15   20

90%
70%
50%
30%
10%

% of bond's value that is deferred interest

deferred interest and you expected your tax rate to change in 10 years, you could find the intersection of 50% and 10 years in Figure 15-3, see it's in the light area, and decide it would be better to cash in your HH bonds now, pay the tax on the deferred interest, and buy Series EE or I bonds.

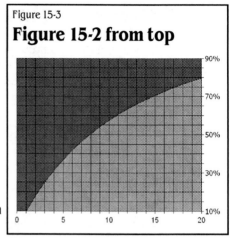

Figure 15-3

Figure 15-2 from top

However, keep in mind that Figures 15-2 and 15-3 also assume that the EE/I bonds will average just 2.5% and that your tax rate will drop from 35% to 28%.

To help you find the best action for other tax rate changes, the following figures show the effect of a variety of drops in your tax rate under three different assumptions:

★ Figure 15-4 – the new Series EE or I bond you reinvest in pays an historically-low average rate of 2.5%

★ Figure 15-5 – the new bond pays an historically-mid-dling average rate of 4.5%

★ Figure 15-6 – the new bond pays an historically-high average rate of 6.5%

As you can see from the graphs, keeping 1.5% Series HH bonds almost never makes sense. If it does make sense, it's because:

★ Your tax rate will fall drastically while you hold the Series HH bonds
★ Your tax rate will fall sooner rather than later
★ The value of the bonds you hold now is primarily interest
★ The Series EE/I bond interest rate remains at historically low levels

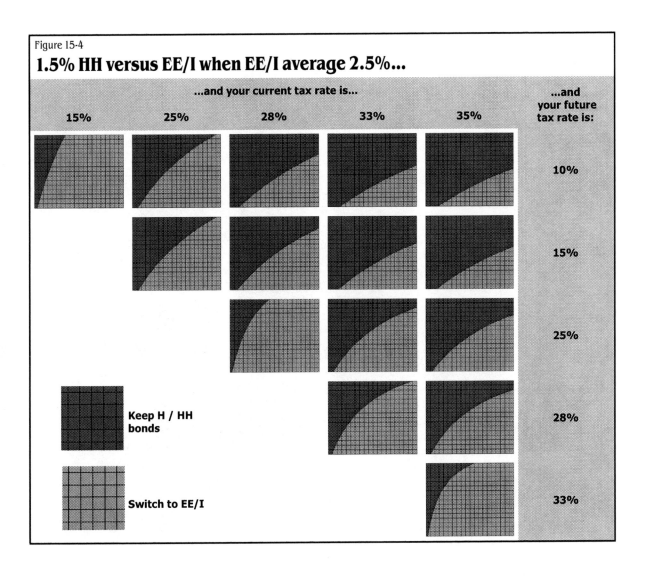

Figure 15-4
1.5% HH versus EE/I when EE/I average 2.5%...

...and your current tax rate is...

...and your future tax rate is:

15%   25%   28%   33%   35%

10%

15%

25%

Keep H / HH bonds

28%

Switch to EE/I

33%

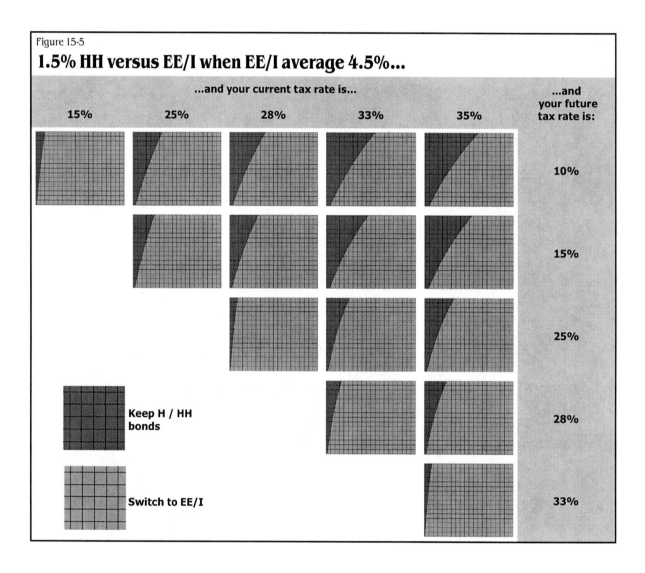

Figure 15-5

1.5% HH versus EE/I when EE/I average 4.5%...

...and your current tax rate is...

...and your future tax rate is:

15%	25%	28%	33%	35%	

10%

15%

25%

Keep H / HH bonds

28%

Switch to EE/I

33%

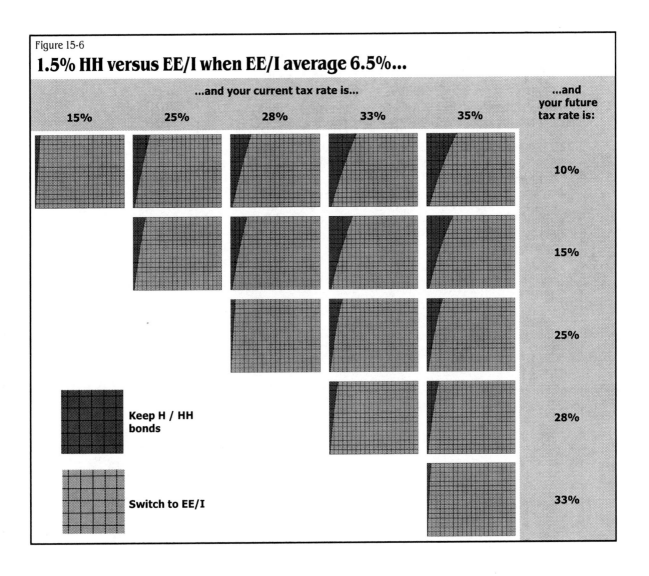

Figure 15-6

1.5% HH versus EE/I when EE/I average 6.5%...

...and your current tax rate is...

| 15% | 25% | 28% | 33% | 35% |

...and your future tax rate is:

10%

15%

25%

Keep H / HH bonds

28%

Switch to EE/I

33%

What if you need the current income of Series HH bonds?

Before TreasuryDirect, there was no way to get current income from Series I or EE Savings Bonds. If you own Series HH bonds, on the other hand, the Treasury will deposit the interest you've earned in your bank account every six months.

Now you can get current income from Series I or EE bonds by using TreasuryDirect's partial withdrawal feature. As long as you withdraw $25 or more and the issue month you're withdrawing from has a remaining balance of at least $25, there are no limits on TreasuryDirect's partial electronic withdrawals.

The withdrawals can be scheduled, they can be increased in months in which you need extra money, and they can be lowered in months when you don't. This makes TreasuryDirect EE or I bonds a lot more flexible than HH bonds in terms of income.

Note, however, that you can't make withdrawals during the first year and there is a three-month interest penalty on withdrawals made before five years.

What if you hold 4% Series H or HH Savings Bonds?

If you now hold Series H or HH Savings Bonds, you may be earning 4% rather than 1.5%. All Series H bonds that are still paying interest and all Series HH bonds pay 4% except:

★ HH bonds issued from January 2003 through August 2004

★ HH bonds that have turned 10 years old since January 2003

If the fixed base-rate on Series I bonds was 2.5% or more, or if the Series EE bond rate was above 4.5%, it could make sense to switch out of even 4% HH bonds. Neither rate is that high however, so it makes sense to hold on to these bonds.

Depending on the size of your investment and the amount of free money you're getting from tax-deferment, you may want to convert a few bonds each year to avoid the effects of the deferred-tax time bomb.

As we've seen in this analysis, you'll do better with the HH bonds when:
  ★ Interest rates on Series EE and I are historically low
  ★ Your tax rate will go down – the sooner the better
  ★ Your bonds carry a high proportion of tax-deferred interest

Chapter 16

Basics of Savings Bond redemption

How to cash in a Savings Bond

Avoiding hidden interest-rate penalties

How much do I hold back for taxes?

Redemption tips for Series I Savings Bonds

Redemption tips for Series E / EE Savings Bonds

Redemption tips for Series H / HH Savings Bonds

How to cash in a Savings Bond

The simplest way to redeem a paper Savings Bond is to take it to a financial institution that handles Savings Bond transactions. In most states this includes most banks, savings and loan associations, and credit unions, but it's best to call ahead to make sure.

The basic process is similar to cashing a check. A bank representative will ask you for identification. Then you will sign your name on the back of the bond and the bank representative will certify your signature.

Remember that you must be the owner or co-owner of the bond to redeem it. However, a parent can sign for a minor child if the child is the owner of the bond.

In some cases you won't receive your money immediately from the bank, but the bank can begin the transaction for you.

Electronic Savings Bonds can be redeemed online through your TreasuryDirect account. The proceeds are deposited into the bank account you specify.

Both paper and electronic Savings Bonds can be partially redeemed. For TreasuryDirect's electronic Savings Bonds, you must redeem at least $25 and you must leave at least $25 in the account for that specific issue date. For paper Savings Bonds you must redeem an amount that can be split between what you receive in cash and a bond with a smaller denomination.

Special case redemption form

If you want to redeem a large number of bonds or if you have any difficulty getting your signature certified at a local bank (for example, if you aren't a US citizen and have no plans to come to the US), you can submit **Public Debt Form 1522**, *Special Form for Request of Payment of United States Savings and Retirement Securities Where Use of a Detached Request is Authorized.*

To get a copy of this form, go to our web site and click on Book Note 16-1.

Don't forget that you can pay hidden interest-rate penalties when you cash in Savings Bonds.

The information in this chapter will help you avoid making that mistake.

If you don't have internet access, you can order a copy of this form by mail. See the Appendix for complete instructions.

Otherwise, see Book Note 16-1.

With this form, you can provide a list of the bonds – the list must include serial numbers – and have your signature certified on the form rather than on the back of all of the bonds. In other cases the form and its instructions will provide a way to have your signature certified when that is otherwise a barrier.

If you can't find a bank that will redeem your Savings Bonds, you can send them to the Federal Reserve for redemption – but the bank still has to certify your signature on the back of the bonds or on Form 1522. See the Appendix for more information.

Bonds less than a year old

In general, you cannot redeem Savings Bonds that are less than one year old. However, after a natural disaster, such as a flood, hurricane, or tornado, the Treasury sometimes allows those who have been impacted to redeem these newer bonds.

If you are in an area that has been affected by a disaster, you may be eligible. There's a page on our web site that tracks when the Treasury makes this option available; see Book Note 16-3.

Whether you've been in a disaster or not, you will pay a three-month interest penalty if you redeem a Series I or EE Savings Bond before it's five years old.

Fifth anniversary bump

Because of the three-month penalty, Savings Bonds have a much larger-than-usual increase in value when they arrive at their fifth anniversary. If you have a Saving Bond that is almost five years old, you should avoid redeeming it until its fifth anniversary if you can.

When everything is equal, you should redeem bonds that are more than five years old first. However, things are at times unequal – then it makes sense to keep older bonds that are paying a higher rate or that are earning free interest through tax deferral even if you have to pay the three-month penalty on newer, lower-rate bonds.

If a bond owner is unable to go to bank to have his or her signature certified, the owner can give a durable power of attorney to someone else who can. There's a link to a form, which the owner will still have to have signed by a notary public, on our web site. Click on Book Note 16-2.

Book Note 16-3 will take you to the page on our web site that lists disasters for which the Treasury has lifted the one-year Savings Bond holding period

Avoiding hidden interest-rate penalties

As I just mentioned, when you redeem a Series EE or I Savings Bond before it's five years old, you lose the most recent three months interest the bond has earned.

However, you can lose up to six months interest on bonds older than five years by simply cashing them in on the wrong day.

All Series E bonds, all Series H and HH bonds, and Series EE bonds issued before May 1997 pay interest - and therefore increase in redemption value - just twice a year.

On the other hand, the newer Series EE bonds issued in May 1997 and since, and all Series I bonds, increase in redemption value monthly (however, for the purpose of calculating how much interest you've earned, interest is added to the value of all Savings Bonds semiannually, not monthly).

When the redemption value of your bond increases just twice a year, you need to redeem the bond right after an increase. Otherwise you lose all the interest from the day of the increase to the day you redeem the bond.

Every month, some Savings Bond holders unwittingly lose nearly six months worth of interest by redeeming right before their bond's value increases.

Redeem Saving Bonds on the first business day of the month in which interest is paid – otherwise you will lose the interest for the days between the first business day and the day you actually redeem the bond.

Purchase Savings Bonds, on the other hand, near the end of the month – you'll earn the same amount of interest no matter which day of the month you invest.

The increase in value occurs on the first business day of the month in which the bond was issued and six months later.

Use Table 16-1 to determine when to redeem your Savings Bonds.

Table 16-1

When to redeem to avoid hidden penalties

Series I **Series EE issued May 1997** **and since**	Redeem on the first business day of any month.
Series EE issued April 1997 **and before** **Series E** **Series H** **Series HH**	Redeem on the first business day of the month of issue or of the month six months later.

How much do I hold back for taxes?

When you redeem a Savings Bond, the Treasury notifies the IRS of the amount of interest you have earned on a 1099-INT tax form. You'll be issued a copy of this form – sometimes when you cash the bond, but usually the following January.

If you redeem an electronic bond, log into your Treasury-Direct account to get your 1099. If you redeem a paper bond, look for one in the mail.

The interest earnings you receive in cash – the amount shown on the 1099-INT – are your pre-tax earnings. Your after-tax earnings will be less than this.

Many people either reinvest or spend the entire amount they receive when they cash a Savings Bond. When tax time comes the following April, they don't have any money to pay the tax bill with.

Don't make this mistake!

Back in Chapter 14, Table 14-1 gives you the percentage of your Savings Bond interest that you should reserve for your tax payment.

You can keep this amount in a bank account until tax time to earn a bit of interest or you can remit it immediately as an estimated tax payment.

At tax time, you will owe the IRS a penalty for underpayment if:

★ you owe more than $1,000 when you file your return and
★ your withholding and estimated tax payments are less than both 90% of your current-year taxes and 100% of your previous year taxes

Depending on how much Savings Bond interest you've earned, it can make sense to send what you'll owe on your Savings Bond interest to the IRS immediately as an estimated tax payment to avoid a tax penalty.

How to make an estimated tax payment

You can make an estimated tax payment by mailing the IRS a check and a Form 1040-ES payment voucher or by using the Electronic Federal Tax Payment System (EFTPS).

If you already file Form 1040-ES, just add the amount you'll owe for your Savings Bond interest to your next payment. On the other hand, if this is the first time you've filed Form 1040-ES, Book Note 16-4 will link you to the instructions and payment vouchers.

Book Note 16-4 is a link to IRS Form 1040-ES.

If the only thing you have to pay is the tax on your Savings Bond interest, you can skip the 1040-ES worksheet and go straight to the payment vouchers. There are four of them – the difference is the due date printed in the upper-right corner of the vouchers.

Pick the voucher that has the next upcoming due date, write in the amount of tax you'll owe (multiply the interest you've earned by your marginal tax rate from this book's Table 14-1), and send it in.

Book Note 16-5 is a link to EFTPS, which is shown in Figure 16-1.

The Form 1040-ES instructions will tell you where to send the voucher and your payment. It also has a version of the marginal tax rate table that our own Table 14-1 is based on.

Alternatively, you can enroll in EFTPS and have the money deducted from your bank account. Book Note 16-5 has a link to EFTPS.

On your first visit, click on the **Enrollment** button. After you have heard back by mail that your account is ready, just click on the **Make a Payment** button to initiate an estimated tax payment.

Figure 16-1

EFTPS online tax payment system

Redemption tips for Series I Savings Bonds

Table 16-2 lists every issue of I bond, its fixed base-rate, and our Alert Recommendation for that issue. Alert Recommendations use letter grades like the one you got in school. If you want to redeem some, but not all, of your I bonds, redeem the ones with the lowest Alert Recommendations first.

The fifth-year anniversary bump isn't included in the Alert Recommendation – consider that aspect of your bonds in addition to the Alert Recommendation.

Table 16-2

Series I – Alert Recommendations

Issue Date	Months spanned	Fixed base-rate	Alert Recommendation
Sep 98 – Oct 98	2	3.40%	A+
Nov 98 – Oct 99	12	3.30%	A+
Nov 99 – Apr 00	6	3.40%	A+
May 00 – Oct 00	6	3.60%	A+
Nov 00 – Apr 01	6	3.40%	A+
May 01 – Oct 01	6	3.00%	A+
Nov 01 – Oct 02	12	2.00%	A
Nov 02 – Apr 03	6	1.60%	B+
May 03 – Apr 04	12	1.10%	B
May 04 – Apr 05	12	1.00%	B
May 05 – Oct 05	6	1.20%	B
Nov 05 – Apr 06	6	1.00%	B
May 06 – Oct 06	12	1.40%	B

Redemption tips for Series E / EE Savings Bonds

Table 16-3 lists every issue of Series E and EE bonds and our Alert Recommendation for that issue. Redeem bonds with the lowest Alert Recommendations first.

The fifth-year anniversary bump and hidden interest rate penalties – covered earlier in this chapter – aren't part of the
- Alert Recommendations – take those aspects of your bonds into account in addition to the Alert Recommendation when deciding which bonds to redeem.

Table 16-3

Series E / EE – Alert Recommendations

Issue Date	Months spanned	Original maturity guarantee / fixed rate	Alert Recommendation
1941 – 1976	428		Interest stopped – stinker alert
1977	12		Stops paying interest in issue month
Jan 78 – Feb 78	2	Original maturity guarantee complete – these bonds are worth more than their face value	A (Because of their age and high lifetime yield, these bonds are earning an extra, hidden 0.5% to 2% from tax deferral)
Mar 78 – Apr 78	2		
May 78 – Feb 83	57		
Mar 83 – Apr 83	2		
May 83 – Apr 84	12		
May 84 – Feb 93	117		A-
Mar 93 – Apr 95	26	18 years – 3.89%	B
May 95 – Apr 97	24	17 years – 4.12%	B+
May 97– May 03	73		A
Jun 03 – Apr 05	34	20 years – 3.50%	A-
May 05 – Oct 05	6	3.50%	B-
Nov 05 – Apr 06	6	3.20% (20 years – 3.50%)	C
May 06 – Oct 06	6	3.70%	B-
Nov 06 – Apr 07	6	3.60%	B-

Redemption tips for Series H or HH Savings Bonds

Unlike other series of Savings Bonds, Series H and HH bonds don't have a three-month interest penalty when they are redeemed before five years. In addition, the minimum holding period for H and HH bonds is history so all are now redeemable.

On redemption, you will receive the face value of the bond. However, the principal owner (not the person who cashes the bonds, as with other paper Savings Bonds) will also receive a 1099-INT tax form showing the amount labeled *deferred interest* on the face of the bond. This is the deferred interest from the Series E or EE bonds that were converted into Series H or HH bonds.

Keep in mind that the deferred interest can create a deferred tax time bomb (see Chapter 14). It's best to redeem these bonds in amounts that don't raise your tax rate.

All Series H and HH bonds also have the hidden interest-rate penalty discussed in the first section of this chapter.

Financial institutions are sometimes reluctant to get involved in cashing Series H and Series HH bonds because they don't deal with them regularly. If this happens to you, turn to the Appendix and use the method described there to have your bonds cashed by the Federal Reserve.

When you have to decide which Series HH bonds you will redeem, consider the interest rate that each of your bonds is currently paying, how long each bond will pay that rate, and when each bond will mature. On the next page, in Table 16-4, you'll find our current recommendation for which Series H and HH Savings Bonds to keep.

Table 16-4

Series H / HH – Alert Recommendations

Issue Date	Months spanned	Current rate	Alert Recommendation
1952 – 1976	296	0%	Interest stopped – stinker alert
1977	12	4.0%, then 0.0%	Stops paying interest in issue month
1978 – 1979	24	4.0%	A
1980 – 1986	84	0.0%	Interest stopped – stinker alert
1987	12	4.0%, then 0.0%	Stops paying interest in issue month
1988 – 1992	60	4.0%	A
1993 – 1996	48	1.5%	D
1997	12	4.0%, then 1.5%	Rate drops in issue month
1998 – 2002	60	4.0%	A
2003 – 2004	20	1.5%	D

Chapter 17

How to minimize the income tax bite

The stinker bond penalty

The double-taxation trap

The state income tax deduction

The education deduction

Using a charitable deduction to avoid taxes

How to avoid the stinker bond penalty

The IRS says you have to pay income tax on a Savings Bond's interest in the earlier of these two years:

★ when your redeem your bond
★ when your bond stops earning interest

Many Savings Bond investors are under the impression that they can avoid income tax by simply not redeeming their bonds.

Or from a kinder, gentler point of view, they just forget about their bonds and don't realize they've stopped earning interest.

Over 5% of the Savings Bonds outstanding have stopped earning interest. As you know by now, I call these stinker bonds.

When you redeem a stinker bond that stopped paying interest in a previous year, you and the IRS can receive a 1099-INT reporting the interest *for the previous year*.

So thanks to this stinker bond, now you're not just giving the Treasury an interest-free loan, but you're:

★ paying the tax you always owed anyway
★ filing an amended tax return for a previous year
★ paying a penalty for underpaying your taxes that year

You can avoid all this by redeeming your bonds as soon as they mature.

Once your tax rate is as low as it's going to get, you should be redeeming a few bonds and paying the tax owed every year. If you don't need the money, reinvest in new bonds.

This avoids not only the stinker bond penalty, but also the deferred tax time bomb I told you about in Chapter 14.

How to avoid the Savings Bond double-taxation trap

The 1099-INT tax form that you and the IRS will receive when you cash in a Savings Bond will always show how much interest the bond earned over its entire life.

This will be true whether income tax has already been paid on some of this interest or not. When the 1099-INT leads you to pay tax a second time, you've been caught in the double-taxation trap.

One situation in which tax on some of the interest may have been paid is when you cash a bond that was originally purchased by someone else. If the bond was a gift that was reissued in your name, the person who gave it to you received a 1099-INT for the interest earned up to the time of the gift.

Likewise, if you were named as the beneficiary on a bond, tax on the interest up to the time of the original owner's death may have been paid by the original owner's estate. Depending on how the estate was handled, sometimes it is but usually it's not.

The second situation in which tax on some of the interest may have been paid is when you have elected to include your Savings Bond interest on your tax return each year. I described a reason to do it this way in Chapter 14.

When you prepare your tax return, if you can demonstrate that some of the tax on a Savings Bond that you've cashed in has already been paid, report the entire interest amount shown on your 1099-INT with your other interest income. Then, as a final interest entry, write *US Savings Bond Interest Previously Reported* and subtract the amount of interest on which tax has already been paid.

If you are audited, you'll have to provide hard proof that the tax was paid. The best proof is a copy of the tax return when the tax was paid – but if you received the bond as a reissued gift or as a beneficiary, that will be someone else's return – and it might be difficult or impossible for you to get a copy.

The lesson is – if you inherit a Savings Bond or if a Savings Bond is reissued in your name as a gift, also ask for the gift of the tax return showing that tax has already been paid on part of the bond's interest earnings. If return's preparer noted the serial numbers of the Savings Bonds on which the tax was paid on the return, that's all the better, although it's not strictly necessary.

If you have paid a significant amount of double-tax within the last three years, you can file amended tax returns to get the money back.

How to avoid state and local income taxes on your Savings Bond interest

The interest you earn from a Savings Bond is exempt from both local and state income taxes.

However, there's nothing automatic about this exemption. To get it, depending on what state you live in, you'll probably have to fill out an extra form when you do your state income taxes. If you have your taxes prepared for you, make sure this happens.

Typically, state income tax forms begin with the adjusted gross income from your federal income tax form. Your Savings Bond interest will be included in this number.

Next, your state income tax form will allow you to enter modifications to the federal adjusted gross income. You will probably have to calculate your modifications on that extra state tax form.

On the extra state tax form, look for a line titled something like *Interest on U.S. Government Obligations* in the section on *Subtractions from Federal Adjusted Gross Income*. That's where you enter your Savings Bond interest. This removes the interest from your official state income so you don't pay tax on it.

But forget this detail, and your state income tax exemption is lost. You'll pay tax that you don't actually owe.

The fine print of the Savings Bond college education deduction

The federal government offers a large number of programs to help you get a college education deduction for yourself or a dependent.

The simple truth is that the ability to deduct Savings Bond interest from your income when it is spent on education is one of the least attractive options.

If you are in the planning stage of figuring out how to pay for college, please realize that books as big as this one are devoted to the subject. A good place to start is with IRS Publication 970, *Tax Benefits for Education*. Go to our web site, and click on Book Note 17-1 for a link to this publication.

The problem with the Savings Bond education interest deduction is that it comes with a large amount of fine print. It's actually impossible to even know whether you'll qualify for the deduction when you start investing.

One way to deal with this is to use your Savings Bonds to fund Coverdell and other qualified tuition-savings programs (QTPs), such as 529 plans, in years in which you know you qualify for the deduction. For many people, this is the best way to take advantage of the Savings Bond deduction.

We discussed another way to fund a college education with Savings Bonds - a method that doesn't even try to use this deduction - in the *When your tax rate is headed up* section of Chapter 14.

However, if you already own Savings Bonds and you have education expenses, you may be able to cash in a bond and deduct at least some of the interest you've earned from your income, if you can meet all of the following limitations:

★ You are the registered owner of the bond

★ If there is a co-owner, it is your spouse

★ Your bond is Series I or Series EE and was issued in January 1990 or later

Book Note 17-1 links to IRS Publication 970, **Tax Benefits for Education.**

★ You were at least 24 years old on the issue date of the bond
(the first day of the issue month)

★ The education expenses are for you, your spouse, or a person
you are claiming as a dependent on this same tax return

★ The education expenses are for:
  ★ tuition and fees (not room, board, or non-degree courses)
  ★ contributions to a qualified tuition program or QTP
  ★ contributions to a Coverdell education savings account
    (ESA – also known as an education IRA)

★ You haven't already used the above expenses for other
income-tax related deductions on this return

★ Your modified adjusted gross income is within the limitations. For the 2007 tax year, the deduction phases out at
the lower end of the ranges shown here and is not available at all to those over the high end:
  ★ Married filing jointly or qualifying widow or widower:
    $98,400 – $128,400
  ★ Married filing separately – deduction not allowed
  ★ All other filing statuses: $65,600 – $80,600

Book Note 17-2 links to a page on our web site that includes the limitations for the last, current, and next year. It's updated annually.

The deduction also phases out if the amount of money
you receive from cashing the bonds (not just the interest, mind
you, but the total amount) is more than the eligible education
expenses. This can be a particular problem if you happened to
invest in bonds with high denominations – you will have to make a
partial redemption for cash and a new bond with a lower value.

Because of this hassle, a new investment program aiming to
take this deduction should be placed in TreasuryDirect's electronic bonds rather than paper bonds, because it's easy to make
partial withdrawals from TreasuryDirect.

There are two tax forms you'll have to fill out to take the
deduction. **Form 8815** calculates the two phase outs and **Form
8818** is an optional form for recording the data on the bonds you
cashed in. We have links to these forms on our web site – see Book
Note 17-3.

Book Note 17-3 links to IRS forms 8815 and 8818, which are needed to take the Savings Bond education deduction.

Using a charitable deduction to avoid taxes

I'm often asked if Savings Bonds can be reissued to charities. They cannot.

However, under certain conditions you can avoid the tax on your Savings Bond interest by donating it to an IRS recognized charity in the year you redeem the bond.

Basically, the way this technique works is that you declare the interest you've earned on your tax return. On the same return, you take a charitable deduction for your donation, which cancels out the Savings Bond interest income.

If you're interested in this technique, there are a few things you need to consider.

First, you can't take a charitable deduction that's more than 50% of your adjusted gross income in any year. If you donate more than that, you can carryover the excess to the following tax year, but there are several arcane rules associated with this.

Moreover, for some organizations, such as veterans organizations, fraternities, cemeteries, and some private foundations, the limit is 30% of your adjusted gross income rather than 50%.

There may also be associated tax issues, such as the Savings Bond interest income making your Social Security income taxable or snaring you in the Alternative Minimum Tax.

If you think this might work for you, see **IRS Publication 526**, *Charitable Contributions*. Then consult your tax advisor.

There's a link to this IRS publication at Book Note 17-4.

Appendix

Appendix

Contacting the Treasury

Dealing directly with the Federal Reserve

Index

Contacting the Treasury

The Treasury unit that handles Savings Bonds is called the Bureau of Public Debt (BPD). The BPD contracts out Savings Bond purchase and redemption transactions to the Federal Reserve Bank, which is a separate governmental unit from the Treasury. The BPD handles all other transactions – registration changes, lost bond searches, setting and calculating interest rates – itself.

The BPD doesn't advertise any phone numbers or email addresses, but you can contact them using a form on their web site. They will answer your question by email, or you can use the form to send them your phone number and a good time to call you back and they will.

Book Note 18-1 links to the BPD contact form.

Book Note 18-1 links to an online form you can use to contact the Bureau of Public Debt, the Treasury unit that handles Savings Bonds.

How to obtain the forms you need

In the text of this book I mention a number of forms the Bureau of Public Debt uses for Savings Bonds transactions. Next to each reference, I give a link to our web site, where you can get a free electronic (Adobe Acrobat .pdf file) copy of the form.

If you would prefer to use a pre-printed form, go to our web site, click on Book Notes, and select note 18-2. This will link you to an online order page on the Treasury's Savings Bond web site that allows you to order free paper forms and have them mailed to you.

Book Note 18-2 links to a Treasury web site where you can place an online order for free paper copies of the forms mentioned in this book.

When you're at the Treasury's form ordering page, select the number of forms you want on the left side of the form, then scroll down to the bottom of the page, enter your shipping address, and click the **Order** button. There is no charge for the forms you order.

Our other form links take you to electronic copies of the forms that you can print out yourself.

If you would prefer to order by mail instead of using the Treasury's web site, send your name and address and a list of the forms you need, including both the Bureau of Public Debt form number (PDF #) and the name of the form. Send your request to:

Savings Bond Form Request
Bureau of the Public Debt
P. O. Box 1328
Parkersburg, WV 26106-1328

Dealing directly with the Federal Reserve

If financial institutions in your area don't handle paper Savings Bonds, it's possible to work directly with the Federal Reserve.

Where to mail your request

The Federal Reserve has designated two of its offices to handle all Savings Bonds *investment* and *redemption* transactions.

(Note that requests other than investment and redemption – such as requests to have lost bonds replaced or to have a Savings Bond's registration updated – should be sent to the Bureau of Public Debt, not to the Federal Reserve. Those forms have the mailing address you should use printed on the form itself.)

When dealing with the Federal Reserve, enclose a brief letter explaining your transaction. Make sure to include your name and mailing address. Your phone number is also helpful in case of a problem with your transaction.

Send your letter and the completed material described below to the Federal Reserve office that serves your part of the country:

In the West
Federal Reserve Bank of Minneapolis
P.O. Box 214
Minneapolis, MN 55480

In the East
Federal Reserve Bank, Pittsburgh Branch
P.O. Box 867
Pittsburgh, PA 15230

Purchasing Savings Bonds

For purchases, your best option may be to open an account at TreasuryDirect. To buy paper Savings Bonds directly from the Federal Reserve you need a multi-part form that can't be downloaded.

However, you can have the forms mailed to you at no charge by ordering online or by mail as described earlier in this

Appendix. The names and numbers of the forms are:
- ★ **Public Debt Form 5263** - *Order for Series EE Savings Bonds*
- ★ **Public Debt Form 5263-1** - *Order for Series EE Savings Bonds to be registered in the name of a fiduciary*
- ★ **Public Debt Form 5374** - *Order for Series I Savings Bonds*
- ★ **Public Debt Form 5374-1** - *Order for Series I Savings Bonds to be registered in the name of a fiduciary*

When your form arrives, fill it out, write a check to the Federal Reserve for the amount of your investment, and mail the form and your check to the Federal Reserve bank that handles Savings Bonds in your part of the country.

Redeeming Savings Bonds

For redemptions, you don't need a form, but you need to have your signature certified – on the back of the Savings Bonds you want to redeem – by your local bank.

If the bank is reluctant, make it clear that you plan to send the bonds to the Federal Reserve yourself, that you are not requesting that the bank redeem the bonds, and that redemption is impossible unless a bank certifies your signature.

Since the bank's certification is guaranteeing that you are who you say you are, expect the bank to ask for one or more pieces of identification that match your name on the bond. If you are the beneficiary, you will also have to provide the death certificate of the owner.

If there are more than just a few bonds, rather than certifying each one, it's easier to list all the bonds on **Public Debt Form 1522** - *Special Form for Request of Payment of United States Savings and Retirement Securities Where Use of a Detached Request is Authorized* and have the bank certify your signature on the form rather than on each and every bond.

There's a link to PDF 1522 at Book Note 18-3.

Index

Symbols

LaVergne, TN USA
04 January 2011

210774LV00008B/131-132/A